D. A. O'Sullivan

A Manual of Government in Canada

Or, the Principles and Institutions of our Federal and Provincial Constitutions

D. A. O'Sullivan

A Manual of Government in Canada
Or, the Principles and Institutions of our Federal and Provincial Constitutions

ISBN/EAN: 9783337206307

Printed in Europe, USA, Canada, Australia, Japan

Cover: Foto ©Suzi / pixelio.de

More available books at **www.hansebooks.com**

A MANUAL

OF

GOVERNMENT IN CANADA;

OR,

THE PRINCIPLES AND INSTITUTIONS OF OUR FEDERAL AND PROVINCIAL CONSTITUTIONS.

BY

D. A. O'SULLIVAN, ESQ., M. A.,

Of Osgoode Hall, Barrister-at-Law.

TORONTO:

J. C. STUART & Co., PUBLISHERS, 136 YONGE STREET.

1879.

TORONTO:
PRINTED BY PATRICK BOYLE,
16 Francis Street.

THIS LITTLE WORK

IS,

BY KIND PERMISSION, RESPECTFULLY INSCRIBED

TO

THE HONORABLE EDWARD BLAKE, Q. C., M. P.,

BY

THE AUTHOR.

PREFACE.

In the compilation of the following pages the writer has endeavoured to make a fair use of such materials as were within his reach, in order to effect the object he intended. Preceded by no writer on the subject, and desirous of rejecting such contemporary opinion as was neither judicial nor official, nor otherwise authoritative, he has found the task not at all an easy one. From the number of distinguished Constitutional Lawyers in Canada, and especially in this Province, one might have been justified in the expectation that something more permanent than a speech at the hustings, or a pamphlet in some party issue, would have remained as instructive reading on the subject. As to contemporary opinion, very little of it is entitled to grave consideration.

It is needless to say that the writer has carefully avoided using any public expression of opinion, no matter how authoritative it may appear, unless it bore the stamp of some authority with it. In regard to decisions of the Courts and judicial *dicta* on the subject, the former *must* of course be taken to be law; the latter carry weight proportionately with the reputation and ability of the particular Judge pronouncing them. It must be admitted that a Judge, in construing our Constitutional Act, or any section of it, or any Statute in fact, familiarizes himself necessarily with the spirit of the Act; and if he goes out of his way to express an uncalled for opinion, or what may be deemed uncalled for, it is certainly because on that point he has no doubt whatever. Judges have plenty to do in deciding in the disputes immediately before them ; and it is to be expected that before commenting on any foreign subject they generally will have entertained strong views on it. The writer makes no apology for regarding such *dicta* as entitled to great consideration ; and only regrets that he was unable to find more judicial utterances in the Law Reports than are incorporated herein.

The utterances of any of our public men, speaking in their official capacity as servants of the Crown and Country, are deserving of consideration next only to what must be regarded as settled law. The writer has faith in the political morality of our leading statesmen to the extent, at least, that no one of them, acting in an official or, as may be said, a judicial position—as advisers of the Crown, as trustees of the Constitution—would permit his judgment to be biased by a mere party spirit, or for a temporary party triumph.

If it be otherwise in Canada, then it is time we were governed without party, as that term is now understood.

Accordingly, all official papers and correspondence, both of English and Canadian Ministers while in office, bearing on the subject, have been freely used.

None of the other sources need comment.

In his task the writer has consulted no one, and asked no one's opinion. It is only fair to state this, as it may well happen that in a work which was the joint production of the writer and others, any excellence in it would be attributed to them and the defects to himself. Whatever there is in this book deserving either of praise or blame, is attachable to the writer, and to no other person.

It was originally intended to make the work complete for each Province as to the Executive Departments, and to add the Courts of Law thereto. This was abandoned, partly because some necessary information from professional gentlemen in the other Provinces did not come to hand in time, and also because, if rumor be true, a description of the Courts in Ontario as they are now constituted, may not apply for any length of time.

Some other alterations were made in the plan of the work after portions of it were in type.

The indulgence of the public will have to be asked in regard to any errors in this edition. Though in contemplation for some time, it was entirely remodeled and re-written within the past two months; and it was put through the press very rapidly.

The writer acknowledges with pleasure the assistance he has received, both in the preparation of the Index and otherwise, from Mr. C. L. Mahony and Mr. A. A. Archbold, Students-at-Law.

Toronto, December, 1879.

PLAN.

TABLE OF CONTENTS.

—◆——

LIST OF AUTHORITIES

USED IN THE IMMEDIATE PREPARATION OF THIS WORK.

BAGEHOT—The English Constitution.

BLACKSTONE's Commentaries.

BOURNE'S Story of Our Colonies.

CHALMERS' Opinions of Distinguished Lawyers.

CHITTY on the Prerogatives of the Crown.

CLARK's Colonial Law.

COOLEY's Constitutional Limitations.

Cox's British Commonwealth.

FINLAYSON's History of the Privy Council.

HALLAM's Constitutional History of England.

HODGINS' Voters' Lists.

LATTEY's Privy Council Practice.

MACFIE's British Columbia and Vancouver's Island.

MARTIN on the Colonies.

McDONALD's British Columbia and Vancouver's Island.

McGREGOR's British America.

ORDERS in Council—Imperial, Dominion and Provincial.

POMEROY's Constitutional Law.

REPORTS of English and Canadian cases in the Privy
Council, Supreme and Provincial Courts.

RULES of the Senate, Commons, and the Provincial Assemblies.

SEDGWICK's Constitutional Law.

SESSIONAL Papers—Dominion and Provincial.

STATE Papers and Opinions of Officials on Constitutional
points.

STATUTES—Imperial, Dominion and Provincial.

WATSON's Constitutional History of Canada.

INTRODUCTORY.

THE following pages are intended for the assistance of those who are unacquainted with the machinery of Government in Canada, and who are anxious to know something of its Constitution, its powers and its objects. It is not to be expected that within the limits of a few hundred pages it could be of assistance to those whose attention has already been turned to the subject ; and that, therefore, it would be a book to refer to on disputed or doubtful points of Constitutional Law. It will satisfy the expectation of the writer if it can be made to fill a want in our schools and colleges, or if it sometimes supply information to the legal student on points where the lack of Canadian authorship may have left him in ignorance. When the elementary knowledge contained in the following pages is as well known to the youth of this Province as the Geography or Grammar taught in our schools, one may reasonably hope that an elaborate and exhaustive work on the Canadian Constitution may find some writer willing to grapple with the subject, and not a few readers who are already posted on its fundamental points. The aim of this little HAND BOOK is to furnish such information on the manner in which we are governed as every student should know, and to furnish it in as plain language as the subject will permit in the hands of the Author.

It is beyond question that in our schools and colleges, and even in our universities, nine-tenths of the students

and graduates are almost in utter ignorance of any
accurate knowledge of the Constitution under which
they live, or of the machinery of State which makes,
expounds or carries into execution the law of the land·
This is certainly to be deplored ; and the cause of it
lies mainly in the fact that there is no elementary
Canadian work which is accessible to them, or which is
made a part of their education. The aim of the present
work is to place the frame-work of the Constitution of
Canada before the young public and to draw their
attention to the process of making laws and carrying
them into execution.

The learned reader bearing this in mind need not,
therefore, expect much more in the perusal of the
following pages than without which is ignorance indeed.
What the position of affairs is conceived to be will
be stated in the writer's conclusion drawn from the
authorities on the subject; but no speculations will be
attempted as to the solution of the many difficult
questions that can, and no doubt will, arise under our
Constitution. A treatise on these questions must be
left for other hands, and will then be addressed to a
different class of readers to that intended to be reached
by the present one.

In this connexion it may be necessary at the outset
to define some terms used hereafter, which may prevent
any confusion of ideas on the subject. In order to
obtain an exact notion of a term much used—
that is the *Constitution*—the young student is asked
to regard the people of this country in the light of two
classes or bodies—the governing body or rulers, and
the governed. The rulers and the ruled both form
the people who agree with themselves, or a portion of

themselves rather, as to the manner in which they are
to be governed. This agreement or understanding
between a people and their masters is their Constitution; and so by the Constitution of Canada is meant the
agreement the people have with themselves as to the
manner in which the Government of the country is to
be carried on. Of course, Canada being a dependency
of Great Britain, any such agreement must have been
necessarily submitted to and approved of by the
Mother country—she having a voice in the matter.
In a free State or Nation, however, the people are the
source of all power; and when they determine on the
manner in which they are to be governed, on their
Constitution in fact, they are final and supreme judges
of their own mode of Government. What has been
said will explain the meaning of another word. *Government*, which is ambiguous and capable of creating
much confusion in its different applications. In its
true and broad sense, Government means the carrying
out of the Constitution—the task of governing the
people according to the understanding had with them.
In Canada, as in England, the task of carrying on the
Government of the country is, by the terms of the
Constitution, entrusted to persons called Ministers of
the Crown, who are collectively called the Government.
This important body is also styled the *Ministry* or
Administration, and sometimes the Cabinet or Cabinet
Council, but their proper appellation here is the Queen's
Privy Council for Canada. Reference will be made
hereafter to the strict use of these terms, it being
sufficient for the present to state that the Government
of the country, using Government in its broad sense, is
carried on by the assistance and on the advice of Privy

Councillors, properly so-called. Government being effected by *laws*, these Councillors are responsible for all laws that are enacted. They provide means for the interpretations of these laws or statutes, and it is their duty to see that the laws are carried into effect. These are the three functions of Government—its Legislative, its Judicial and its Executive functions. So far as its judicial functions are concerned, they are carried out by means of judges appointed for that purpose. When the Privy Council, instead of carrying on portions of the Government by means of Judges, administer themselves directly, it is called administrative Government, and is a branch of the Executive. The acting Privy Councillors are then usually called the Administration from this fact.

The Privy Council or Administration have, therefore, the whole task of Government in their hands; but in every step they take they must have or count on the support and approval of *Parliament,* and especially of that portion of Parliament called the Commons, who represent and are elected by the people. The Administration is answerable to the people through the Commons, and this is what is meant by Responsible or Constitutional Government. When an Administration does not govern the people as they want, the people can turn them out of office at the next elections, and send in Commoners to support an Administration in accordance with the popular will. A double safe-guard in Canada is that the persons composing the Administration must either be Senators, or must be elected as Commoners, in order to entitle them to fill the position of members of the Administration.

The science or the art which treats of the government or the administration of the national or public affairs of the Country is called *Politics.*

The policy or acts of any particular Administration, when viewed as beneficial to the country or otherwise, are called Politics also, but more properly Party Politics· It is a discussion and criticism on the Administration, and on its supporters—the party in power, the ruling party, usually upholding their acts ; and the party not in power, the Opposition, being adverse thereto.

These short definitions, it is to be hoped, will not be considered out of place before the subject in hand is taken up. No attempt is made at elaborate exactness in defining these terms : all that is intended is to give a comparatively correct notion of them without misleading the reader.

In order to prepare the student for viewing the Constitution of Canada as it is, a chapter will first of all be devoted to what it has been in some of its previous phases of existence.

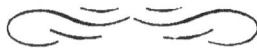

CHAPTER I.

Up to the middle of the last century nearly the whole of North America was owned partly by England and partly by France. England lost a large portion of her possessions by the revolt of the thirteen colonies in 1776, when the Declaration of Independence of what are now the United States was signed, and these colonies severed their connexion with the Mother Country. Prior to this, in 1760, France lost her Dominion in the New World, not to the Colonists, but to the English, who captured Quebec; and this French territory the English yet retain, and is included in the Dominion of Canada of to-day. The inhabitants, numbering between sixty and seventy thousand, were mostly French Canadians. For three years the Colony was governed under military rule of the English, but the French laws were administered. Canada being a colony by cession, its new masters had a right to impose such laws on it as they chose, subject to any treaty that might be had between the contending parties. In February, 1763, the Treaty of Paris was signed; and by it Canada, with all its dependencies, was ceded to Great Britain. By a proclamation in October following, Quebec was to have a Governor

in the person of General Murray. Promise was
made for the summoning of a General Assembly
to aid in the government of the Province; but
this promise was in reality a dead letter, as no
Assembly was ever called.

The Governor and his Council administered
English laws to a Colony of French Canadians, and great dissatisfaction was the result.
In 1774 the Colonists presented petitions in
England for the redress of their grievances.
In that year the Quebec Act was passed, which
made matters far worse. The Royal Proclamation of 1763 was revoked, and so the French
laws were left in force, except as to criminal
matters, upon which the law in England was
to rule.   An Advising Council, whose ordinances were binding, except as to the imposition of taxes or duties other than for public
roads and buildings, was organized; but no
Assembly, to be elected by the people, was
granted in this Act. The Council consisted of
not more that twenty-three members, and every
ordinance made by them was subject to be disallowed by the King.   The Quebec Act, denying
the Colonists any share in their own Government, was disliked by the Canadians and other
North American Colonists; and, indeed, it was
one of the Acts of the Mother Country which
drove the latter to assert their independence.
Canada, however, remained loyal to Great Britain, though not without frequent murmurings

at the irresponsible Government under which the Colony was ruled. In 1776 the other British Colonies broke away from Great Britain and formed themselves into the United States, as has been already mentioned.

It was not till 1791 that England became alive to the importance of conciliating the Canadians, and of granting them a Constitution under which they could have a share in their own government. In that year what is known as the Constitutional Act (31 Geo. III., cap. 31) was passed, and in it the Quebec Act was repealed and a Constitution granted to Canada. By its provisions the Province of Quebec was divided into Upper and Lower Canada for the English and French settlers. The boundary between the Provinces was then determined, and remains the same till the present day. Ample machinery for the government of each Province was provided in the persons of Lieutenant-Governors, Houses of Assembly, and Legislative Councils. The Lieutenant-Governor appointed the members of the Council; the people elected the members of the Assembly. In Upper Canada the Legislative Council was composed of not less than seven members, who held their seats for life. The members of the Legislative Assembly in Upper Canada held office for four years. In Lower Canada the Legislative Council was composed of not less than fifteen members; the Legislative Assembly of thirty members. The Houses sat every year, and before any measure became law it was necessary that it should be approved of by the King.

The first Legislature for Upper Canada, under Lieutenant Governor Simcoe, met on the 18th of September, 1792, at Niagara. All the procedure of the British Parliament was imitated as nearly as could be by a very young colony, and in the very unpretentious log building provided for the assembled legislators. Certainly no Provincial Legislatures so nearly approached in constitution the pattern from which they were taken as the mimic Parliaments of Niagara and Quebec under the Constitutional Act of 1791 ; for their Lieut.-Governors and Commoners were scarcely any less than those of the present day—their Legislative Councillors were more than our Senatorial dignatories. A hereditary right to sit in the House was in some cases recognized, similar to the Peerage in England, though this transplanting of aristocracy did not seem to thrive in a new country.

The new Provincial Legislatures made such laws as were approved of in England. All laws in force before 1791 were to be effective till altered or replaced by the new legislatures. The first proceeding in Upper Canada was to make the law of England the law of this country in all things relating to property, civil rights, and trial by jury, thereby remedying the Act of 1774 as applied to British subjects. This Act is more important, however, in a legal than in a constitutional point of view. Several other important Acts were passed in the first session, notably the one abolishing slavery.

The Act of 1791, though in a great measure remedying the difficulties that two races offer to the legislator, was only a step towards self-government. Notwithstanding the assumptions of Parliamentary power the Provincial Legislatures possessed little of the omnipotence of even a Colonial Parliament. The power of disallowance in the King was in theory at all events a possible check on the most popular Act emanating from the Colony, and in practice it gave rise to murmurings and discontent. The Lieutenant Governor and his appointees, the Legislative Council, were in effect the disallowing parties; and it became a question who should govern the Provinces—the members of the Assembly elected by the people, or the irresponsible advisers of the Crown.

This form of our Constitution lasted for fifty years in Upper Canada, but was suspended in the lower Province at being found impossible for the two houses to work harmoniously. The struggle for Responsible Government, which culminated in deeds of violence in both Provinces began early in both. It was not, however, till 1838 in Upper Canada that the Home Government took steps to remedy the existing evils. Then the

British Government again took up the question of Colonial Government, and what was called the Union Act of 1841 was passed, by which Upper and Lower Canada were united into one Colony, with one Legislative body for both Provinces. Under the new Constitution given by this Act the benefits of Responsible Government were accorded for the first time to British Colonists in America. Laws for both Provinces were enacted in a Legislature which sat alternately in Toronto and Quebec—sixty-two members representing each Province. Of these 42 were elected by the people, and 20 appointed by the Crown as Legislative Council. After fifteen years experience of this form of representation a new feature was introduced. The Provinces were divided into electoral districts—48 for each—and a representative elected for each district, twelve to go out at the end of every two years. This gave only partial satisfaction; and besides, a number of things occurred to make the problem of discovering a suitable Legislature for the Provinces difficult of solution. The differences of race, of religion, were as frequently difficulties in the way of harmonious government as at any time since the cession. The seat of Government was also no trifling matter of arrangement. Up to 1844 it was part of the time in Toronto and in Kingston. After 1849, when it was removed from Montreal, the Legislature sat alternately at Toronto and Quebec.

In 1857 the project of Confederating the British possessions adjoining the Canadas was taken up. After a number of conferences and resolutions four out of six Provinces agreed to a union on a federal basis, which came into force in July, 1867. The object of the following pages is to give some idea of the details of the new Constitution under the British North America Act of 1867. It is the sixth change that has taken place for the old Colony of Canada since 1760 :

1. Military Government of General Murray, 1760-1764
2. Civil Government by Governor and Council, 1764-1774
3. Government under the Quebec Act 1774-1791
4. Government under the Constitutional Act. 1791-1841
5. Government under the Union Act 1841-1867
6. Government under the B. N. A. Act 1867

No references could fairly be made here to the negotiations and conferences which led up to the Union of 1867. The result was a new departure in Colonial Government—the Provinces, retaining control over a great part of their Local concerns, were federally united into one Dominion or Colony, which legislated for them on all other subjects.

Of the constitutional history of Nova Scotia and New Brunswick, prior to their admission into the Federation of 1867, but little need be said. Nova Scotia, formerly Acadia, was a Province of France up to 1713, when it was ceded by the Peace of Utrecht to Great Britain. In 1758, a Constitution was granted it ; and by it a

Governor, a Legislative Council, and a Legislative Assembly, made laws for the Province. Nova Scotia comprised also the Island of Cape Breton. New Brunswick, prior to 1784, was also part of this Colony. The first Legislative machinery of New Brunswick was similar to that of Nova Scotia, except in the peculiarity that the Executive Council of the Lieutenant-Governor, consisting of twelve members, possessed Legislative capacity. The Constitution of these Provinces remained the same after the passing of the British North America Act, except as to certain points noticed hereafter.

Prince Edward Island was taken possession of by the English in 1758. After the treaty of Paris the Island and Cape Breton were annexed to the Government of Nova Scotia, and afterwards separated. The Island had the same form of Government, prior to its admission into the Federation of the Provinces in 1873, as Nova Scotia.*

The Governor of Canada was Captain General of British America, but did not interfere with the administration of the other Colonies. These were presided over by what were called Lieutenant-Governors, though they were governors in everything but name, being commanders-in-chief within their provinces and taking precedence next after the Governor of Canada.†

* See Clark's Colonial Law. McGregor on British America. Howard's Colonial Law.

† See McGregor's British America.

British Columbia and Vancouver's Island were formerly part of the Hudson Bay Territory. The latter in 1848 was assigned to the Company for ten years, and about the end of that time it and the mainland were taken away from the Hudson Bay Company and formed into separate Colonies. In 1866 they were united under one administration. Previously in 1863 a Royal Governor was sent out and a Government formed, one half of the advising Council being composed of Government officials and the other half elected by the people of the Colony.*

Manitoba and the North-West Territories had no separate political existence before forming part of Canada. They were portions of Prince Rupert's Land, ceded to Canada by the Home Government.

---

* See Macfie's British Columbia, Macdonald's British Columbia, or Bournes' Story of our Colonies.

CHAPTER II.

THE Constitution under which we in Canada live and are governed is a new departure in the history of Colonial Government. We have glanced over the various experiments made by the Provinces now composing the Dominion of Canada in the solution of satisfactory government; and they are generally seen to be composed of a Governor, a Legislative Council, and a Legislative Assembly for each Colony or Province. Most of these Colonial possessions were heretofore all outlying fragments of the Empire, with no cohesion and no nationality, with nothing in common except the tie to the Mother Country. The scheme of uniting the Provinces had been long in contemplation. It was felt that at least everything which they had in common might well be decided in one central legislature ; and that if one body could not direct all the affairs of the different Provinces, they could manage such interests as were not antagonistic. The example of a great and prosperous Republic was at hand as evidence of the success, or at least the possibility of a Federacy, where each State managed its own local concerns, but delegated certain powers to a Central Government, to be held and exercised by them in trust for the whole Union. There were, on the other hand, the traditions of the Government of Great Britain, which are the inheritance of all her present and past Colonies. The present Constitution is the result—the unintentional result, perhaps —of a Federal system somewhat analogous to that of the United States, so far as the distribution of legislative power is concerned, and yet being very different from it in the underlying principle of its Constitution. Like the States of the Union, the Provinces of the Dominion are united for some purposes, and separated for others. There is a federacy—a union for matters of general and, one might say, national interest; there is a separation for matters of local or internal interest.

This, however, is probably the only point of resemblance between Government in Canada and in the United States; and it will be seen presently that there is a great difference even in the distribution of these powers. The study of the United States Government becomes somewhat useful in regarding our own, which is indeed a a mixture of British principles and of Institutions unknown in the British Constitution, but familiar in the United States.

A Republican form of Government, such as exists in the United States, has in theory little in common with the British form of Government. The similarity of President, Congress and Representatives at Washington to the Queen, Lords

2

and Commons at London is apt to be misleading. The theory of Government is totally different in each, and the distribution of power to Local and Central Legislatures has no counterpart in Great Britain. The fact that the Government of Canada has Local Legislatures and one central one, and is in principle the same as the Government of Great Britain, makes a consideration of both forms necessary to a Canadian student. It is mainly in reference to the distribution of Legislative power that a study of the United States is of value, although our Judiciary has functions very analogous to theirs in regard to questions of Constitutional Law.

The principle of English and Canadian Government is theoretically that the Sovereign is the source of power. The Queen is the head of the Parliament, or chief legislative power; the executive power is vested in her, and the judicial power emanates from her as Chief Magistrate of the nation. The Sovereign is the apex—the summit of the triple power. Practically the House of Commons in England controls the Parliament or legislative power, directs the executive and appoints the judiciary—the Sovereign being satisfied with the leader in the House of Commons. So far it is the same in Canada.

In the United States the powers are divided up, and do not point to any one source. The Executive Government is vested in the President; and unlike the British Sovereign, he exercises it personally and is a real power in himself. The Legislative power is possessed by the Senate and the House of Representatives, and the Judiciary is vested in the Supreme Court of the United States and in the other Congressional Courts throughout the Union.

It may be safely said that the Executive power is the same here as in England ; the Legislative and Judicial powers are more nearly allied to those exercised in the United States, although the source of both is different.

First, as to the Legislative power :

When the present Constitution of the United States was formed, one theory at all events in regard to the distribution of Legislative power, was that the separate States of the Union surrendered to the United States Government a portion of their sovereignty, and retained all the residue of it to themselves. This portion was given to the Central Government absolutely and irrevocably. The Local Governments kept the reserved powers to themselves—the Central Government was one of enumerated powers. Every power not expressly given to the Central Government was reserved to the Local Government. The powers of both were derived from the same source—the people—and it would require the people to act before these powers could be altered.

The action of the Separate Colonies of Great Britain, which now form Canada, was somewhat

similar ; but the principle of surrendering their
Legislative powers is just the reverse of what it is
in the United States.   The Provinces surrendered
all their Legislative powers to the Central
Government, reserving for themselves the power
to Legislate on certain specified subjects.   With
us the enumerated powers are with the Local
Governments ; the reserved powers are with the
Central Government.   Every power not expressly
given to the Provinces is given to the Dominion
of Canada.   Both powers were derived from the
same source—the British Legislature ratifying
the will of the people of Canada—and these
powers cannot be altered but by that same
power.

In framing both Constitutions the grand problem was to divide up the powers between the
Local and Central Legislatures in the best possible way for the country.   If the Local Governments got too much power there would be little
use in a Federacy—the Central Government
would be a shadow—a useless piece of expensive
machinery.   If the Central Government got too
much, there would be a cry that local independence was gone—that it would be as well to have
one Government only—that the Local Legislatures were mere municipal bodies with but few
powers and of little importance.   The division
of the legislative power by the fathers of Confederation in Canada has not been the cause of
discontent or jealousy.   The reserved powers

were properly left to Canada, as well as all matters of general interest and matters in which
uniformity in legislation is desirable. The Provinces have not complained of an unequal distribution ; and if there is anything to complain
of, they may blame themselves. The Dominion
and the powers of its Parliament are the creation
of the Provinces. They allotted the distribution
before the Dominion existed.

Second, as to the Judicial power :

The duties of the Canadian Courts are relatively of more importance than those of the British Courts. In England the powers of the
Legislature are, so far as human power can be,
omnipotent. Its acts are superior to judicial
interpretation, so far as the question of their
constitutionality is concerned. In Canada the
Courts are in a different position. Its humblest
tribunal may declare an Act of Parliament unconstitutional, and may refuse to follow it.
There can be no restraint put upon the due
exercise of the judicial power by any authority,
Dominion or Provincial ; for that would be to
place these bodies above the law which created
them and granted them powers which are not
absolute, and which no legislation of theirs can
make so. *

A Provincial Legislature may trench in the
limits of the Dominion, and the Parliament of
Canada may usurp local rights. In either of
these cases the courts must declare whether the

---

* Regina v. Taylor, Mr. Justice (now Chief Justice) Wilson.

legislative bodies have transcended their powers, and may declare acts of this nature unconstitutional and void.

A similar judicial power exists in the United States. The Supreme Court is the most important judicial tribunal in the world. It is the supreme arbiter of the nation under the constitution.

A consideration of the foregoing will give some idea not only of the difficulty of forming a right notion of the complicated system of government in its different divisions that obtains amongst us, but will also furnish us with a proper notion of the importance of Canada presiding over her Provinces and Territories.

" Canada," says one of her most distinguished statesmen, " is not merely a Colony or a Province. She is a Dominion composed of an aggregate of seven large Provinces, federally united under one Imperial charter, which expressly recites that the Constitution is to be similar to that of the United Kingdom. Nay, more : besides the power with which she is invested over a large part of the affairs of the inhabitants of the several Provinces, she enjoys absolute power of legislation and administration over the people and Territories of the North-West, out of which she has already created one Province. and is empowered to create others, with representative institutions." *

---

* Hon. E. Blake, Minister of Justice, to the Earl of Carnarvon, 1876.

CHAPTER III.

The Imperial Act, known as The British North America Act, 1867, settled and defined the present Constitution of Canada. For several years previous to that date, as has already been intimated, the question of uniting portions of the British possessions in America was actively discussed. After a number of concessions from all parties the points of agreement were laid before the British Parliament. and a written Constitution drafted thereon. The late Province of Canada, comprising Upper and Lower Canada, and the Provinces of Nova Scotia and New Brunswick were federally united into one Dominion—Canada—under the Crown of the United Kingdom of Great Britain and Ireland, with a Constitution similar in principle to that of the United Kingdom. By it one PARLIAMENT, consisting of the Queen. an Upper House, styled the Senate, and the House of Commons, was given to Canada. The Executive power of and over Canada was continued, and is vested in the QUEEN. A Privy Council to aid and advise in the Government of the country was established, and an officer styled the Governor-General, who possesses all the powers, authorities and func-tions of our former Governors, so far as they can

apply under the Act, represents her Majesty
the Queen, and carried on the Government in
her name and on her behalf. The SENATE was
a body appointed by the first Governor-General,
and intended to be as permanent as in the
nature of things they could well be. The members of the House of COMMONS were to be elected
by the votes of the people as their representatives. These three constituent elements of our
Parliament, corresponding to the Queen, Lords
and Commons in England, are to be expected,
when it is remembered that the principle of the
Colonial and Imperial Parliaments was intended
to be the same. Here, as in England, the chief
Executive Power is declared to be vested in the
Queen, but limited by the two houses of Parliament. The basis of the British Constitution is,
that the power of making, abrogating, changing
or explaining its laws belongs to Parliament
alone. Bearing in mind the power of disallowance lodged in the Governor-General and in the
Queen, there is no doubt but that the Canadian
Parliament has, under its Constitution, a parallel
authority. Neither in England nor here does
the Legislative power reside in the Crown,
though the latter possesses the whole power of
carrying out the laws. The desire of the guardians of both Constitutions is said to be to keep
the exercise of the Legislative and Executive
powers as distinct as possible from each other.
In effect, however, they are linked together, as

will be seen hereafter. The power of the Crown being limited by its Constitutional advisers, the form of Government is called a limited Monarchy. The power of the Crown in England was declared in 1688 to be derived from a contract with the people. The people owe allegiance to the Crown, and the Crown grants protection in return. The Crown represents the nation—is supreme Magistrate, appoints judges, distributes honors, receives and sends ambassadors, makes treaties, declares war, summons and dissolves Parliament. But all acts of the Crown must be advised and transacted by ministers responsible to the people. and the King or Queen must govern according to law.*

In Canada the Royal Authority is the same as in England—Royalty here acting through a representative. The contract with the people in the Constitution is traceable to the cession of Canada by the Treaty of Paris in 1763, and re-acknowledged in various ways since, chiefly by the Act of Confederation, which was the work of the people's representatives. But the functions of a Governor-General, though representing Royalty, are more restricted than those appertaining to Royalty itself. His duties do not involve many international offices—he has no ambassadors to send, and Canada as a Colony has none to receive. There are no treaties to be made nor wars to be declared; but it is probable

---

* Cox's British Commonwealth.

that all the prerogatives of Royalty necessary to
a Colony are exerciseable by him, and attached
to his person and office.

The SENATE, though corresponding largely to
the House of Lords in England, yet differs in
many respects from the latter body. The
absence of a titled aristocracy in Canada, to
which the members of our Upper House may be
supposed to belong, is one chief feature. The
duration of their Patents, the limit to the term
of holding office, the restriction as to their
numbers, the absence of judicial functions, are a
few of the points of difference between them.
The chief uses of both bodies may be said to be
the same—to prevent hasty legislation, and be in
composition a body fearless of wrathful constituents and an equipoise to preserve the balance
of the Constitution.

The third estate in the realm, the COMMONS,
has fewer points of dissimilarity than either of
the other two. The Commons, under a constitutional form of government such as we possess,
are the important part of Parliament. The
Privy Council, if not mainly of their number,
report in their House as to the manner of conducting the Government. The supplies for
carrying on all government originate with them.
They are in fact the *people*—the supreme ruling
power.

With us, as in England, the concurrence of
these three elements of Parliament is necessary

to every measure. All must act in concert in order to produce a law. If the Lords in England should refuse to act harmoniously with the Commons, new Peers of the realm could be created in accord with the popular wish. If the Commons could not agree with the Lords, the former could be dissolved and new members elected by the people. But the last power would generally be found to be with the Commons, who have virtually, in England at all events, the determining of the law in their own hands. In Canada, in case a deadlock were to occur between the Senate and the Commons, there could very well arise cases for which no remedy is at hand. The number of Senators cannot be increased but by a very small number, which may be still too small to command a majority ; and if the Commons and Senate remained obstinately in opposition to each other the Government could not go on. It would be necessary to have an Imperial Act passed to make legislation possible and the work of Government continue.

In case the Senate and Commons agree, Bills may be reserved by the Governor-General for the signification of the Queen's pleasure, or he may withhold the Queen's assent. Our position as a Colony gives rise to the former case. The latter has no counterpart, in practice at least, in England. There, if a Bill be passed in the Lords and Commons, the Queen does not now refuse her assent thereto, the power of veto having fallen into disuse. Here, if a Governor-General refused the Queen's assent to a Bill, it would be equivalent to an intimation to the Ministry to resign—that he refuses to take their advice. While possessing the undoubted right to refuse the Queen's assent to any Bill, a Canadian Governor-General will scarcely ever refuse the Queen's assent, but adopt the other course of reserving it for Her Majesty's pleasure in the event of its being objectionable.

The peculiar feature of the British Constitution in its Cabinet, or PRIVY COUNCIL, has been already noted. The Privy Council would seem to mean the present and past advisers of the Crown. In practice, however, the past advisers, who are usually in Opposition, do not tender advice till called upon in a change of Ministry. The Cabinet Council here, as in England, means the Ministry or Administration for the time being—the Government, in fact, of the day.

The task of Government is carried on by an Administration so long as they can command a majority in the two Houses of Parliament, and are the choice of the Crown. This is what is meant both in England and here by responsible government. Parliament here has no judicial functions, nor does any of its branches form an Appellate Court, as in England. When a change of Ministry occurs by the action of Parliament, its action is administrative. The functions of Canadian Parliaments otherwise are mainly

legislative, and in this respect the Parliament of
Canada is limited to certain specified subjects
under the Constitution.

These will be referred to hereafter. In Great
Britain the Parliament is the supreme ruling
power—it represents the sovereignty of the
British people.

In all Colonies there is a division of the sovereign power, part of it being exercised by the
Colonial Legislature and the remainder by the
Imperial Legislature. In Canada there is a
threefold division of sovereignty—part of it
Imperial, part Canadian, and part Provincial.
These, although they all exist and are exercised
within the same territory, are yet separate and
distinct sovereignties acting separately and
independently of each other within their respective spheres.*

Every subject proper to be legislated for in
Canada falls either within the sovereignty of the
Provinces or of the Dominion. In two instances,
that of Immigration and Agriculture, it may
fall within both. In matters where Imperial
interests are in question it is likely to fall within
neither.

Other points of difference in the Constitutions
are mainly in details, and arise from difference
of position. The English Constitution is for the
most part unwritten. Some few of the great
props, such as the Magna Charta, the Bill of

---

* See Cooley on Constitutional Limitations.

Rights, the Act of Settlement, are embodied in Acts of Parliament with the other laws of the land.

The Dominion has, in fact, a written and defined Constitution, but it is not limited by it. It possesses powers which are neither defined nor limited, excepting by the Confederation Act and the Imperial Statute 28 and 29 Vic., ch. 63. It has general sovereignty in all matters but those in which it is expressly excluded, or in which, from the inherent condition of a dependency, it is necessarily and impliedly restricted.*

---

* Mr. J. (now C. J) Wilson, Regina v. Taylor, 36 U. C. R.

THE first constituent element of the Parliament of Canada is not only in principle, but is in reality the same as the first element of the Parliament of the United Kingdom. This is the King or Queen of Great Britain and Ireland, who is the first estate in the realm.

In Canada the King or Queen is represented by a Governor-General, who is appointed by the Secretary of State for the Colonies. He holds office during the pleasure of the Sovereign of Great Britain ; and in the event of the Sovereign's death, for six months after that date, in case no new appointment is made. An administrator or other officer may be appointed to carry on the Government of Canada on behalf of and in the name of the Queen, and all the provisions of the Confederation Act, in reference to the Governor-General, apply to such administrator, or under whatever other title he may be known. The Queen may authorize the Governor-General to appoint any person or persons jointly or severally to be his Deputy or Deputies, within any part or parts of Canada, and the Governor-General may assign to such Deputy or Deputies, to exercise during his pleasure, such powers, functions and authorities of the Governor-

General as the latter may deem necessary or
expedient to assign to him or them, subject to any
limitations or directions expressed or given by
the Queen.   Any such appointment, however,
does not affect the powers, authorities and
functions of the Governor-General himself.
The death of the Governor does not dissolve
the Parliament.   It is called to consult with the
Queen, and not with him ; and there might be
ten Governors during the reign of one Queen,
with the same Parliament assisting at the last
as well as the first.   He is not the *caput princi-
pium et finis* of the Colonial Constitutions.*

The Governor General chooses and summons
his Privy Councillors, and removes them when
the Government of Canada requires it.

He also summons in the Queen's name, by
instrument under the Great Seal of Canada,
persons of necessary qualifications for Senators.
At the time of the Union of the Provinces in
1867, Lord Monck, the first Governor General of
the Dominion of Canada, inserted the names of
the Senators in the Queen's Proclamation of the
Union of the four Provinces.   Any additional
Senators are hereafter to be summoned by the
Governor-General ; and whenever a vacancy
happens in the Senate by resignation, death or
otherwise, the Governor-General fills the vacancy
by new appointments of qualified persons.

He also appoints a Speaker to the Senate, and

* Chalmer's Opinions.

may remove and appoint another in his place. The Speaker must be a Senator ; and in this particular the Senate, as to that officer, differs somewhat from the Speaker of the House of Lords in England, who is not necessarily a Peer of the realm—or member of the House of Lords. But in case he is not a Peer, he is not entitled to vote or take part in the debates in the House.

The Governor-General summons and .calls together the House of Commons in the Queen's name, and may dissolve the same within the period of five years from its commencement. Independent of this statutory provision the prerogative right in relation to the dissolution of General Assemblies is at least as extensive in the Colonies as it ever was in England. In respect to the English Parliament and this prerogative of the Crown, whatever the extent of it may be, every Governor by his Commission is empowered to exercise in his particular Province.*

He is empowered to assent in the Queen's name to Bills passed in both Houses. He may also refuse the Queen's assent to such Bills, or he may reserve the Bill for the signification of the Queen's pleasure. He also, when the Queen's pleasure is signified on a reserved Bill, declares by Speech or Message to the Houses, or by Pro- clamation, that it has received the assent of the Queen in Council. Copies of all Bills assented to are sent to one of the Secretaries of State, and

---

* Chalmer's Opinions.

3

may be disallowed at any time within two years. He must recommend to the House of Commons all money bills. He originates no measure, and by himself has no Legislative powers. He has a negative voice only in the Legislature.

The Governor-General appoints the Judges for the Superior, District and County Courts, except the Judges of the Probate Court in Nova Scotia and New Brunswick, and may remove Judges of the Superior Courts on address of the Senate and House of Commons. He has also, until the Parliament of Canada otherwise provides, the appointment of such officers as may be deemed necessary and proper for the effectual execution of the Confederation Act. An appeal lies to the Governor-General in Council from any act or decision of any Provincial Authority in reference to Separate or Dissentient schools in relation to Education affecting the rights and privileges of any supporters of Separate or Dissentient schools. In case Provincial law seems to the Governor-General in Council requisite for this purpose, and that it is not made by the proper authorities; or in case the proper Provincial authorities do not duly execute the directions of the Governor-General in Council in any such appeal, the Parliament of Canada may legislate thereon.

The Governor-General in Council appoints a Lieutenant-Governor for each Province under the Great Seal of Canada, and may appoint an Administrator to execute the office and functions of Lieutenant-Governor during the absence, illness or other inabilities of the latter ; and the Governor-General* may remove a Lieutenant-Governor within five years from his appointment on assigning cause for such removal. The Governor-General in Council may disallow acts of a Provincial Legislature within one year after their enactment in the same way as the disallowance of an act of the Parliament of Canada is signified in England, except that in the latter case two years are allowed to pass instead of one.

The power of the Governor-General in Council to disallow a Provincial Act is as absolute as the power of the Queen to disallow a Dominion Act, and is in each case to be the result of the exercise of a sound discretion, for which exercise of discretion the Executive Council for the time being is, in either case, to be responsible, as for other acts of Executive Administration.†

The twelfth section of the British North America Act relates to the general powers of the Governor-General, and is as follows :

* In some parts of the Act of 1867 certain powers are given to the Governor General in Council, and in other parts to the Governor General, omitting the words *in Council*. This arose, it is said, from adopting the language of older Acts under which the Governor General had unmistakeable powers apart from or independent of his Council. Before the era of Responsible Government in Canada the Governor General by himself had large administrative powers, and the phrase Governor General had a different significance from what it has now. The Council was then an irresponsible body ; so long as they agreed with the Royal representative they cared little for the popular element. The popular element now controls the Council, and it is apprehended that any acts of a Governor General for which an existing Ministry is to be called to account by the people, must be done on the advice of his Council, no matter whether so expressed or not. See Sir John A. Macdonald's letter to Sir Michael Hicks Beach on the Letellier question, and the Hon. Edward Blake on the Royal Instructions to Lord Dufferin as to exercise of Prerogative of Pardon by a Governor General.

† Per C. J. Harrison in Leprohon v. Ottawa, 40 U. C. R.

" All Powers, Authorities, and Functions which, under any Act of the Parliament of Great Britain, or of the Parliament of the United Kingdom of Great Britain and Ireland, or of the Legislature of Upper Canada, Lower Canada, Canada, Nova Scotia or New Brunswick, are at the Union vested in or exerciseable by the respective Governors or Lieutenant-Governors of those Provinces, with the Advice, or with the Advice and Consent, of the respective Executive Councils thereof, or in conjunction with those Councils, or with any number of Members thereof, or by those Governors or Lieutenant-Governors individually, shall, as far as the same continue in existence and capable of being exercised after the Union in relation to the Government of Canada, be vested in and exerciseable by the Governor-General, with the Advice or with the Advice and Consent of or in conjunction with the Queen's Privy Council for Canada, or any Members thereof, or by the Governor-General individually, as the Case requires, subject nevertheless (except with respect to such as exist under Acts of the Parliament of Great Britain or of the Parliament of the United Kingdom of Great Britain and Ireland) to be abolished or altered by the Parliament of Canada."

The Acts of the Parliament of Great Britain which could relate to this subject are 14 Geo. III., cap. 83, and 31 Geo. III., cap. 31, both of which have already been referred to as the Quebec Act of 1774 and the Constitutional Act of 1791.

There is nothing in the Quebec Act further than repealing the Proclamation of October, 1763, as to the Provisional Government and all the powers and authorities given to the Governors.

In the Constitutional Act, 1791, there is for the first time a Governor or Lieutenant-Governor given to the Provinces of Upper and Lower Canada, into which the former Province of Quebec was divided. The powers of the Governor or Lieutenant-Governor under this Act were as follows :

(1) Bills passed by the Legislative Council and Assembly of the Provinces were, before becoming law, to be assented to by His Majesty, or, in his name, by the Governor or Lieutenant-Governor of the Provinces.

(2) It was lawful for His Majesty, by instrument under the sign manual, to authorize and direct the Governor or Lieutenant-Governor to summon the members of the Legislative Council —seven in Upper Canada and fifteen in Lower Canada—and also such other persons to the Council as he may think fit.

(3) It was lawful for him to summon and call together the Legislative Assembly.

(4) It was lawful for him to divide the Provinces into Districts, to appoint Returning Officers and the time and place of holding elections.

As to assenting to Bills, he declared such assent according to his discretion. but only subject to the Act. He could withhold his assent, or reserve it for His Majesty's consideration.

A feature of this Act is that the Royal instructions to three of the former Governors—Guy Carleton. Sir Frederick Haldimand and Lord

Dorchester—in reference to tithes and the support of clergy were incorporated into the Act.

The Union Act 3 & 4 Victoria, cap. 35 (1840), an Act of the Parliament of Great Britain and Ireland, has two sections bearing upon this subject. Sec. 40, as to the Authority of the Governor, is as follows :

"Nothing herein contained shall be construed to limit or restrain the exercise of Her Majesty's Prerogative in authorizing, and notwithstanding this Act, and any other Act or Acts passed in the Parliament of *Great Britain*, or in the Parliament of the United Kingdom of *Great Britain* and *Ireland*, or of the Legislature of the Province of *Quebec*, or of the Provinces of *Upper* or *Lower Canada* respectively, it shall be lawful for Her Majesty to authorize the Lieutenant Governor of the Province of *Canada* to exercise and execute, within such parts of the said Province as Her Majesty shall think fit, notwithstanding the presence of the Governor within the Province, such of the powers, functions, and authority, as well judicial as other which before and at the time of passing of this Act were and are vested in the Governor, Lieutenant Governor or Person administering the Government of the Provinces of *Upper Canada* and *Lower Canada* respectively, or of either of them, and which from and after the said Re-union of the said two Provinces shall become vested in the Governor of the Province of *Canada;* and to authorize the Governor of the Province of *Canada* to assign, depute, substitute, and appoint any person or persons, jointly or severally, to be his Deputy or Deputies within any part or parts of the Province of *Canada*, and in that capacity to exercise, perform, and execute during the pleasure of the said Governor such of the powers, functions, and authorities, as well judicial as other, as before and at the time of the passing of this Act were and are vested in the Governor,

Lieutenant Governor, or Person administering the Government of the Provinces of *Upper* and *Lower Canada* respectively, and which from and after the Union of the said Provinces shall become vested in the Governor of the Province of *Canada,* as the Governor of the Province of *Canada* shall deem to be necessary or expedient: Provided always, that by the appointment of a Deputy or Deputies as aforesaid, the power and authority of the Governor of the Province of *Canada* shall not be abridged, altered, or in any way affected, otherwise than as Her Majesty shall think proper to direct."

Sec. 59 of the same Act reads :

" All powers and authorities expressed in this Act, to be given to the Governor of the Province of Canada, shall be exercised by such Governor in conformity with and subject to such orders, instructions, and directions as Her Majesty shall from time to time see fit to make or issue."

The Imperial Enactment, 17 and 18 Vic., cap. 118 (1854), which altered the Union Act, has no important reference to the powers of Governor. It defines the word " Governor" as comprehending the Governor, and in his absence, the Lieutenant-Governor, or person authorized to execute the office, or the functions of the Governor of Canada.

Of the numerous references made to the Governor of the late Province of Canada, in the Statutes, from the Union till Confederation, no detailed reference could be made here. They refer to the necessary duties of Chief Executive Officer of the Province, entrusted with carrying on the Government under the Constitution. In one place we find him made a Corporation sole

—has power of issuing Proclamations, Commissions, &c. In 1845 an Act was passed relating to Commissions, in the first section of which it was enacted that in the demise of the Crown no new Commissions need issue, but a proclamation continuing all public officers in their place should be sufficient. Section 2 is as follows :—" Nothing in the next preceding section shall prejudice, or in any way affect the rights or prerogative of the Crown, with respect to any office or appointment, derived or held by authority from it, nor prejudice, or affect the rights, or prerogatives thereof in any other respect whatsoever." Power is expressly reserved to Her Majesty in an Act passed in the same year to prorogue or dissolve the Provincial Parliament of Canada on the demise of the Crown.

The foregoing will give some idea of the Statute Law, on the powers of a Governor-General; and it is to this, rather than to anything else, that recourse must be had in order to discover what are his powers, authorities and functions. Such prerogative rights of the Crown in England as are called personal rights of the Sovereign, are conveyed to Governors of Colonies only by express delegation. The Royal Commission and Royal instructions generally contain the extent of these.

The Governor of a British Colony is in general invested with Royal Authority, and is the representative and deputy of the British Sovereign. The Sovereign alone exercises the prerogatives of the Crown, and these Royal rights and powers cannot be vested in two persons at the same time. They may and are, however, delegated to Colonial Governors either by the Charter Governments of the Colony or by the Royal Commission and Instructions, but only by express terms. The fundamental rights and principles upon which the Royal Authority rests, and which are necessary to maintain it, extend to the Colonies. The Queen is Sovereign of Great Britain and of the Colonies as well. She has perpetuity, and can do no wrong constitutionally within the British Dominions. The local prerogatives in England, unless by express grant, do not extend to the Colonies : but it seems on good authority that the minor prerogatives and interests of the Crown may be taken up and dealt with by the Colonial Legislatures. Until that happens the prerogative in England prevails.*

This occurred in Ontario where a Lieutenant-Governor was, unless and until authorized by his Legislature, incapable of creating Queen's Counsel —the prerogative of fountain of honor not being within his power under the British North America Act.† This prerogative is, however, vested in the Governor-General, he being the Queen's representative in Canada. The law on the question of prerogative is laid down in Chalmer's Opinions of Eminent Lawyers :

" The prerogative in the Colonies, unless where it is

---

* Chitty on Prerogatives of the Crown.

† The Judges of the Supreme Court appear to differ on this point with the law officers of the Crown in England.

abridged by grants, etc., made to the inhabitants, is
that power over the subjects considered either separately
or collectively, which by the Common Law of England
abstracted from Acts of Parliament, and grants of
liberties, &c., from the Crown to the subject, the King
could rightfully exercise in England."

The Common Law of England on the question
of prerogative is, therefore, the Common Law of
the Colonies on that subject—unless where the
Charter or Royal Commission interposes to extend
or restrict it—and this Law is set out in 17
Edward II., cap. 1, a Statute simply declaratory of
the Common Law. The Governor-General is the
representative of the Queen, and the Queen is
part of our Constitution. Whatever rights are
necessary or exerciseable in a colony must vest
in him as Royal representative, and it is not
material whether they are statutory or prerogative rights.

The Royal Commission and Royal Instructions
are now reduced to the most general terms, and
contain no express delegation of any prerogative
rights.*

When the Governor-General has dismissed
one set of ministers, and is about to choose
another, then, and then only, does he appear
to stand alone under our Constitution. Even
in this case, the new Ministry is responsible
—the Crown is never responsible. The Crown

---

* See the correspondence between the Hon. Edward Blake and the Earl
of Carnarvon as to the Royal Commission and Instructions to Lord Dufferin, and compare the present Commission and Instructions with the last.
Not only Canada but all the British Colonies owe a debt of gratitude to
the distinguished Minister of Justice who successfully pleaded their cause
before the Colonial Secretary on this occasion.

is not supposed to have ministers unless it
accepts their advice. Its independent judgment
seems to be called into requisition when it is
a question as to what party will the reins of
power be entrusted. Once having made a
selection, its acts are the acts of the new
ministry—it is no longer on the Governor-
General's advice, but on theirs, that the country
is governed.

So far as Legislative powers are concerned,
the Governor-General possesses only a negative
voice. The Queen herself cannot be said but by
fiction to possess any such powers, as the first
estate in Parliament would seem to imply. A
measure becomes law in England, it is true,
with her assent, but she would not now refuse
her assent on a measure passed in both Houses.
The two Houses of Parliament could send up a
Bill deposing her, or altering the succession, and
she would be obliged to sign it; and if one
Sovereign refused his or her assent, another
could be got to grant it. As a late vigorous
writer puts it : " She must sign her own death
warrant, if the two Houses unanimously sent it
up to her."* The Governor-General has in the
reservation of Bills a certain power, but beyond
this and his Instructions, and an undoubted
right to refuse advice tendered by ministers, the
principle of the British Constitution leaves in
him as the Queen's representative no positive
legislative powers whatever.

* Bagehot, on the English Constitution.

CHAPTER V.

THE Senate or Upper House is the second element in the Parliament of Canada, and was composed of 72 members when first summoned —24 from Ontario, 24 from Quebec, and 24 from the Maritime Provinces of Nova Scotia and New Brunswick. This number from the Maritime Provinces included their share in the Senate whenever Prince Edward Island was thereafter admitted.

Since Confederation British Columbia has been admitted, and sends three members. Manitoba sends two members until its population, according to a decennial census, attains 50,000 inhabitants, when it may send three; and when the population reaches 75,000 it will be entitled to four representatives in the Senate. The Territories are not yet represented. When Newfoundland is admitted she will be entitled to send four Senators to the Canadian Parliament. The Governor-General may recommend the appointment of three or six Senators, and in case the Queen thinks fit one or two may be appointed from Ontario, Quebec, and the Maritime Provinces.

The number of Senators must never exceed 78, or after the admission of Newfoundland, of

82. There are at present 75 members in the Senate, Ontario sending 24, Quebec 22, New Brunswick and Nova Scotia 10 each, Manitoba 2, British Columbia 3, and Prince Edward Island 4.

The qualifications of a Senator are as follows:

(1) He shall be of the full Age of Thirty Years:

(2) He shall be either a Natural born Subject of the Queen, or a Subject of the Queen naturalized by an Act of the Parliament of Great Britain, or of the Parliament of the United Kingdom of Great Britain and Ireland, or of the Legislature of One of the Provinces of Upper Canada, Lower Canada, Canada, Nova Scotia, or New Brunswick, before the Union, or of the Parliament of Canada after the Union:

(3) He shall be legally or equitably seized as of Freehold for his own Use and Benefit of Lands or Tenements held in free and common Socage, or seized or possessed for his own Use and Benefit of Lands or Tenements held in Franc-alleu or in Roture, within the Province for which he is appointed, of the value of Four thousand Dollars, over and above all Rents, Dues, Debts, Charges, Mortgages, and Incumbrances due or payable out of or charged on or affecting the same:

(4) His Real and Personal Property shall be together worth Four thousand Dollars over and above his Debts and Liabilities:

(5) He shall be resident in the Province for which he is appointed:

(6) In the case of Quebec he shall have his Real Property Qualification in the Electoral Division for which he is appointed, or shall be resident in that Division.

The first Senators were summoned by the Queen by warrant under Her Majesty's sign manual, and their names were inserted in the

Proclamation of the Union in 1867. Thereafter, such persons as were called, and such persons as will be called, to the Senate, were and will be, by the Governor-General, in the Queen's name, by instrument under the Great Seal of Canada.

A Senator, subject to the following provisions, holds his seat for life.

He may, by writing under his hand, resign his place in the Senate.

His seat becomes vacant—

(1) If for Two consecutive Sessions of the Parliament he fails to give his Attendance in the Senate :

(2) If he takes an Oath or makes a Declaration or Acknowledgment of Allegiance, Obedience or Adherence to a Foreign Power, or does an Act whereby he becomes a Subject or Citizen, or entitled to the Rights or Privileges of a Subject or Citizen of a Foreign Power :

(3) If he is adjudged Bankrupt or Insolvent, or applies for the benefit of any Law relating to Insolvent Debtors, or becomes a public Defaulter :

(4) If he is attainted of Treason, or convicted of Felony or of any infamous Crime :

(5) If he ceases to be qualified in respect of Property or of Residence ; provided that a Senator shall not be deemed to have ceased to be qualified in respect of Residence by reason only of his residing at the Seat of the Government of Canada while holding an Office under that Government requiring his Presence there.

Any vacancy in the Senate resulting from resignation, death, or otherwise, is filled by the Governor-General's appointment of a fit and qualified person to fill the vacancy.

Any question arising as to the qualification of a Senator, or to a vacancy in the Senate, shall be heard and determined by the Senate.

No Senator is capable of being elected, or of sitting or voting as a member of the House of Commons.

Every Senator before taking his seat in the Senate must take and subscribe before the Governor-General, or some person authorized by him, a prescribed oath and declaration.

A Senator is entitled to be styled Honorable so long as he is a member of the Senate, and no longer, and he ranks fourth in the precedence assigned to persons in Canada.*

A member of the Senate may be a member of the Ministry or Administration ; and if his duties require him to live at the Seat of Government, it is not necessary that he should reside in his own Province if appointed out of Ontario. No Ontario Senator can be a member of the Local Legislature of that Province.

The Senate is summoned to Ottawa, the Seat of Government, at the same time the Commons is convened. The Speaker of the Senate is appointed by the Governor-General, and must be a Senator, though the analogous course in the House of Lords in England, as was observed, is not followed in this particular. Then the Lord Chancellor is *ex officio* Speaker in the Lords, and is keeper of the Great Seal, but is not necessarily a Peer of the Realm.

---

* See table of precedence hereafter.

Fifteen members, including the Speaker, form at present a quorum for the transacting of business. The Speaker in all cases has a vote. Questions are decided by a majority of votes; and when these are equal, the motion or Bill is lost, or deemed to be in the negative.

The privileges, immunities and powers of the Senate and its members are left to be defined by the Parliament of Canada, but they must never exceed those held by the English House of Commons and its members at the time the Parliament of Canada so defines them.

The rules of the House and the procedure will be shortly adverted to hereafter.

All Bills may issue in this, or in the House of Commons indifferently,* except as to money Bills, which must originate in the Commons. Bills of a judicial nature, such as Divorce Bills, &c., and Bills referring to the rights and privileges of the Senate, would, following the analogy of the practice in the Upper House in England, have their commencement properly in the Senate.

The Senate does not appear to possess any other functions than those of a branch of the legislature, or law-making machinery of the State. In England the Lords possess judicial functions, as well as legislative ones, and their House is the Highest Court for deciding cases referred to it from the English Courts.

The Senate was to be composed of men of

---

* The Senate alone, apparently, takes the initiative in Divorce Bills.

wealth and stake in the country who were superior to party and heedless of local or interested claims. It was thought that to be answerable to constituents was frequently to be obliged to pander to their whims—to legislate for their special interests. This was hoped would be obviated by appointments by the Crown of persons whose own interests would suffer when their country's suffered ; and that the good of the country would even for selfish notions, if for no other, be promoted by them as being largely mixed up with their own individual prosperity. A second House was needed to prevent hasty or inconsiderate legislation—a house wherein the largely increasing legislation for the Provinces could be participated in and matured. It was felt also that some equipoise was needed to maintain the balance of the Constitution.

Any difference between the Commons and Senate here is not so easily adjusted, or rather will not be whenever such a contingency arises. Six members added to the Senate may not be sufficient to make it accord with the majority in the Commons. In 1874 six members were recommended to be appointed, but Earl Kimberly suggested that the Crown would take no action unless a difference had arisen, and that the creation of new members would supply a remedy in the event of an actual collision. Our Senate is in this respect differently situated from the Upper House in England.

4

Such frequent reference has been made to the House of Lords that a few words may be said here of this body, in order to contrast it with the Senate of our own country.

In England the House of Lords is the aristo-cratic element of Parliament, and consists of Lords temporal—that is, lay noblemen or peers, and Lords spiritual—that is, archbishops and bishops. The temporal lords are called Peers of the Realm ; and when of full age, and not imbecile, are entitled to sit in the House in virtue of their titles and ancient rights.

The Lords are in number rather more than two-thirds of the Commoners. A part of them have judicial as well as legislative functions. A special portion of them—all distinguished law-yers, or judges, form the Appellate Court of the House of Lords. Many of them are members of the Judicial Committee of the Privy Council, which is the highest Appellate Court in the Empire for the Colonies.

There are five orders of Peers—Dukes, Mar-quises, Earls, Viscounts and Barons. This is their rank in the order of precedence, but they all sit in the House as Barons, that is, as possessing a barony or landed estate. The Bishops now sit in the House in virtue of their estates, and not in respect of their clerical dignities. They rank before Barons and after Viscounts, and are lords of Parliament, though not Peers of the Realm. The spiritual lords number thirty—the lay lords or peers vary between four and five hundred. This number is maintained by the eldest sons of peers succeeding to their fathers' titles, and also by the Crown creating peers by patent of nobility. The Crown is not limited to the creation of any certain number of peers when a collision happens between the Lords and Commons, but the popular element—the Commons—suggests the appointment of as many as are necessary.

The House of Lords in England may be said to be practically under the control of the Commons. It has the power to delay Bills, and a power to amend them in most cases, but it has no other powers. It can be swamped with new Peers, to make it accord with the ruling party in the Commons, and so cannot stand out against them. When the Commons has made up its mind on any measure, the Lords are powerless to resist. As Bagehot says, their veto is :—" We reject your Bill for this once, or these twice, or even these thrice, but if you keep on sending it up, at last we won't reject it."

The Senate of Canada has larger powers than these. It cannot merely delay Legislation, as it very wisely did in the Insolvency Bill of 1878, but Legislation cannot be got without it. It cannot vote the supplies, but it can vote against the supplies, and put a stop to all Government, as the analogous body, the Legislative Council, foolishly did in Quebec this year. It cannot be

swamped out with new Senators, as the number
at present cannot exceed 78, and never more
than 82, after Newfoundland is a Province of
Canada.   It is not controlled by the Commons,
but must be harmonized with them by administration in accord with their views.   But with
the stake they have in the country, they would
not oppose good Government, and the country
will stand by them in opposing a Ministry with a
ruinous policy.

CHAPTER VI.

THE House of Commons is the third element in the Parliament of Canada, and was originally composed of 181 members representing the four Provinces as follows :

Ontario, represented by .... 82 Members.
Quebec,   "   65   "
Nova Scotia,   "   19   "
New Brunswick, "   15   "

Of the Provinces annexed to Canada since Confederation the following is the representation :

Prince Edward Island, represented by 6 Members.
Manitoba,   "   4   "
British Columbia,   "   6   "

Provision was made at the passing of the Confederation Act for an increase of the number of members in the House, but the proportionate representation of the four Provinces comprising Canada in 1867 must not be disturbed by any such increase. The Parliament of Canada has power as to this increased representation. It was further provided that in 1871, when a census of the people was to be taken, an adjustment of the representation of the four Provinces should take place in Parliament. This gave rise to the

present representation in the Commons, which is
as follows :

Ontario	86	Members.
Quebec	65	"
New Brunswick	16	"
Nova Scotia	21	"
Manitoba	4	"
Prince Edward Island	6	"
British Columbia	6	"
In all	204	"

The different Provinces are divided up into
electoral districts, each of which returns a
member to the Commons on having received a
majority of polled votes in the riding. The
voting takes place by ballot, and all persons
(except Judges in the Court of Chancery for
Ontario, and all other Judges appointed by the
Governor General) qualified to vote at the election of representatives in the Legislative Assembly of the Provinces, and no others, are entitled
to vote at election of members for the Commons.
All lists of voters to be used at the elections in
the Local Houses are to be used for this one also.
The writs for the election of members issue out
of the office of the Clerk of the Crown in Chancery, and are addressed to the Sheriff or Registrar
as Returning Officer in the Electoral District. A
day for the nomination of candidates and the day
and place for holding the polls are then appointed.
Each candidate must deposit $50 with the Return-
ing Officer to apply towards the payment of election expenses. The candidates need have no real
property qualification, but must be either natural

born or naturalized subjects of the Queen. No paid officers of the Crown, except members of the Privy Council holding office, and officers in the Army, Navy, and Militia, and Militiamen (except staff officers of the Militia) are eligible to sit or vote in the Commons.* No contractor with the Government, or any of its public officers, or any of its Departments, is eligible; and no person holding any office, commission, or employment at the nomination of the Crown to which any fee, salary, allowance or profit is attached can be a member of the Commons. No Senator or member of the Local Legislature of Ontario is eligible to sit in the Commons.

Very stringent provisions are enacted in regard to Bribery and Corrupt practices at Elections; and any candidate not returned, or any voter may file a petition complaining of an undue return or undue election of a member, or of no return, or of a double return or unlawful act on the part of the person returned as member; and on notice of the presentation of the Petition being given to the respondent the parties can go to trial on the question, as provided by the Controverted Elections Act. These cases are tried by various Courts in the different Provinces, and an appeal lies therefrom to the Supreme Court at Ottawa.

All the elections, except in a few places, are now made returnable on one day, fixed by the Governor-General, and the various returning

* See Act of 1878.

officers send in their returns to the Clerk of the Crown in Chancery at Ottawa. Thither the members are summoned by Proclamation in the *Canada Gazette*, at the same time as the Senate is assembled. Each member sits for five years, which is the duration of each Parliament, unless sooner dissolved by the Governor-General. Twenty members, reckoning the Speaker, form a quorum for the transacting of business. The members themselves elect their Speaker at the first sitting, and he continues in office during that Parliament, unless a vacancy occurs. When a vacancy occurs in the office of Speaker by death, resignation, or otherwise, it is filled by the House, in the same way as a Speaker is originally appointed. In case of his absence for 48 hours, the House may temporarily appoint a Speaker, who has all the powers, privileges, and duties of the Speaker. The Speaker presides over all meetings of the House, but has no vote, except when the votes are equal. The House of Commons is summoned by Instrument, under the Great Seal of Canada, in the Queen's name, by the Governor-General, at the same time with the Senate. Each member of the Commons must take the oath of allegiance, as a Senator does, before taking his seat in the House. When a vacancy occurs in the Commons it is filled by the issue of a new writ from the Office of the Clerk of the Crown in Chancery for the election of a member for the unrepresented constituency.

CHAPTER VII

SUBJECT to Imperial Authority, the powers of the Parliament of Canada are the general powers of a Sovereign State, excepting those which have been specially conferred on the Provinces.* The effect of Imperial Authority is that the Dominion Parliament has no power to pass any Act, repugnant to the provisions of any Act of Parliament, order, or regulation thereunder, having the force of law in England.+ Such an Act, if passed, would be void and inoperative, but only, however, to the extent of its repugnancy. But a Colonial Act is not void, because it is inconsistent with the Royal Instructions to the Governor-General.

The Sovereignty of a State is defined as extending to everything which exists, by its own authority, or is introduced by its permission. The powers of the Parliament of Canada were introduced by the permission of the people of Canada, and exist by their own authority, ratified by the Mother country. It is different with the Provinces. The powers of their Legislatures are not conferred on them by their own Provinces. but by the people of Canada, with

* Mr. Justice (now Chief Justice) Wilson, in Queen vs. Taylor, 36 U. C. R.

† Imperial Act, 28 and 29 Vic. cap. 63.

the consent of the Sovereign power of Great Britain; and these Provinces cannot confer a Sovereignty which will extend over them, and they cannot be regarded as Sovereign States.*

A portion of the legislative power being reserved to the Provinces, it might have been thought that reserving all other powers to the Central Parliament would have been sufficient. However, the Act for greater certainty declares (91st Sec.) that it shall have exclusive power to legislate for the peace, order and good government of Canada in the following matters:

1. The Public Debt and Property.
2. The Regulation of Trade and Commerce.
3. The Raising of Money by any Mode or System of Taxation.
4. The Borrowing of Money on the Public Credit.
5. Postal Service.
6. The Census and Statistics.
7. Militia, Military and Naval Service, and Defence.
8. The fixing of and providing for the Salaries and Allowances of Civil and other Officers of the Government of Canada.
9. Beacons, Buoys, Lighthouses, and Sable Island.
10. Navigation and Shipping.
11. Quarantine, and the Establishment and Maintenance of Marine Hospitals.
12. Sea, Coast and Inland Fisheries.
13. Ferries between a Province and any British or Foreign Country, or between Two Provinces.
14. Currency and Coinage.
15. Banking, Incorporation of Banks, and the Issue of Paper Money.

---

* Chief Justice Hagarty, in Leprohon vs. Ottawa, 2 App. Ont.

16. Savings Banks.
17. Weights and Measures.
18. Bills of Exchange and Promissory Notes.
19. Interest.
20. Legal Tender.
21. Bankruptcy and Insolvency.
22. Patents of Invention and Discovery.
23. Copyrights.
24. Indians and Lands reserved for the Indians.
25. Naturalization and Aliens.
26. Marriage and Divorce.
27. The Criminal Law, except the Constitution of Courts of Criminal Jurisdiction, but including the Procedure in Criminal Matters.
28. The Establishment, Maintenance and Management of Penitentiaries.
29. Such Classes of Subjects as are expressly excepted in the Enumeration of the Classes of Subjects by this Act assigned exclusively to the Legislatures of the Provinces.

And any Matter coming within any of the Classes of Subjects enumerated in this Section shall not be deemed to come within the class of Matters of a local or private Nature comprised in the Enumeration of the Classes of Subjects by this Act assigned exclusively to the Legislatures of the Provinces.

The construction put upon the wording of the Statute by the late distinguished Chief Justice Draper was that the Parliament of Canada has the right to legislate on the subjects mentioned in the 91st section of the Act to the exclusion of the Imperial Parliament. The exclusive authority mentioned in that section as belonging to Canada does not, he says, refer to the subordinate Provincial authorities, whose powers were not

then conferred in them, but refers to the matters
of which the Imperial Parliament has renounced
its right to legislate thereon.   In support of this
he refers to the two Constitutions given to Canada
in the reign of Geo. III., which empower the
Colonial Legislature to make laws for the "peace,
welfare, and good government" of Canada.   The
present Constitution sets out specifically the
subjects on which the Parliament of .Canada
can deal with, and which may be supposed to
comprise all subjects within the "peace, order,
and good government" of Canada; and in regard
to these the English Legislature has no concern,
and have deprived themselves of the right of
interfering therewith.*   It would appear therefore that neither the Imperial Authorities nor
the Provincial Legislatures have any power to
legislate on any of these subjects.

The Parliament of Canada has moreover
power to make laws for the peace, order and
good government of Canada in relation to all
matters not exclusively assigned to the Provincial Legislatures. In other words, the
Parliament of Canada has power to Legislate on
all such subjects, unless it is expressly stated
that it has not such power.

On the following subjects the Parliament of
Canada has no power to legislate in reference
thereto, but the different Provinces have exclusively this right:

* Regina *vs.* Taylor, 36 U. C. R. See also Crombie *vs.* Jackson, per
Wilson, J. (now C. J.)

In each Province the Legislature may exclusively make Laws in relation to Matters coming within the Classes of Subjects next hereinafter enumerated, that is to say—

1. The Amendment from Time to Time, notwithstanding anything in this Act, of the Constitution of the Province, except as regards the Office of Lieutenant-Governor.
2. Direct Taxation within the Province in order to the raising of a Revenue for Provincial Purposes.
3. The borrowing of Money on the sole Credit of the Province.
4. The Establishment and Tenure of Provincial Offices and the Appointment and Payment of Provincial Officers.
5. The Management and Sale of the Public Lands belonging to the Province, and of the Timber and Wood thereon.
6. The Establishment, Maintenance and Management of Public and Reformatory Prisons in and for the Province.
7. The Establishment, Maintenance and Management of Hospitals, Asylums, Charities, and Eleemosynary Institutions in and for the Province, other than Marine Hospitals.
8. Municipal Institutions in the Province.
9. Shop, Saloon, Tavern, Auctioneer, and other Licenses, in order to the raising of a Revenue for Provincial, Local, or Municipal Purposes.
10. Local Works and Undertakings, other than :—
    a. Lines of Steam or other Ships, Railways, Canals, Telegraphs, and other Works and Undertakings connecting the Province with any other or others of the Provinces, or extending beyond the Limits of the Provinces :
    b. Lines of Steamships between the Province and any British or Foreign Country :

c. Such Works as, though wholly situate within the Provinces, are before or after their Execution declared by the Parliament of Canada to be for the general Advantage of Canada, or for the Advantage of Two or more of the Provinces.

11. The Incorporation of Companies with Provincial Objects.

12. The Solemnization of Marriage in the Province.

13. Property and Civil Rights in the Province.

14. The Administration of Justice in the Province, including the Constitution, Maintenance and Organ- ization of Provincial Courts, both of Civil and of Criminal Jurisdiction, and including Procedure in Civil Matters in those Courts.

15. The Imposition of Punishment by Fine, Penalty, or Imprisonment, for enforcing any Law of the Pro- vince made in relation to any Matter coming within any of the Classes of Subjects enumerated in this Section.

16. Generally all Matters of a merely local or private Nature in the Province.

Within their respective limits each Legislature is apparently supreme and free from any control from any quarter. The Dominion Parliament has no more authority to interfere with or regu- late matters specially assigned to the Provinces than the Provincial Legislatures to regulate matters within the jurisdiction of the Dominion Parliament.*

The powers of the Dominion Legislature and of the Provincial Legislatures are distributed in classes assigned to each. The Provincial Legis- lature having only the powers specifically con-

* Parsons *vs.* Citizen's Insurance Co., 4 Appeal, Ontario, 96, per Burton, J. A. See also C. J. Harrison in Leprohon *vs.* Ottawa, 40 U. C. R.

ferred—the Dominion Legislature having, besides these specifically conferred, all powers not specifically conferred upon the Local Legislatures, it would seem to follow that acts of the Provincial Legislature which conflict with the powers conferred specifically or generally upon the general government are *ultra vires ;* so on the other hand acts of the Dominion Parliament or Government conflicting with powers conferred exclusively upon the Provincial Legislature would be *ultra vires,* would be acts of usurpation. This must result from each being creatures of the one power—each deriving its authority from the same source.*

The Governments of the Provinces are ones of enumerated powers : the Federal Government one of all general powers. A Federal law is presumably valid unless on the list assigned to the Provinces ; a Provincial law is presumably void unless in the enumerated list. The Provinces can claim nothing in the way of legislative powers except what is expressly given to them ; the Dominion can claim everything except what is expressly taken away from it. Within the scope of the functions assigned to each the powers of the central and local governments over the subjects respectively committed to their care are complete, absolute and supreme.┼

Besides this power of exclusive legislation, it

---

* Chancellor Spragge in *Leprohon vs. Ottawa*, 2 Ontario Appeal.

┼ See Pomeroy on the Constitutional Limitation of the States of the Union, in his Constitutional Law.

has power to create new Provinces out of her
Territories, and bestow Constitutions and representative Governments therein, and it may also
legislate for any Territory not included in a
Province.

It has largely to deal with the Judicature of the
country, in the appointment of almost all the
Judges, and it has provisions for establishing a
Court of Appeal for all the Provinces, and any
additional Courts for the better Administration of
the laws of Canada. It can also establish, abolish
and reconstruct Courts of Judicature, and may
alter the Constitution thereof.* It fixes the salaries of the Lieutenant-Governors, and provides for
their payment, and fixes and provides salaries for
nearly all the Judges in Canada. It has control
over the Consolidated Revenue Fund, as to its
appropriation for the Public Service, and it has
all necessary and proper powers with the
Government, for performing the obligations of
Canada or of any of its Provinces, as part of
the British Empire, towards foreign countries,
arising under treaties, between the Empire and
such foreign countries, and it has control of the
Army, Navy, and Defence of the country. It has
concurrent Jurisdictions with the Provinces, in
matters relating to Immigration and Agriculture,
and in case of conflict in this regard, its Statutes
are paramount to the Provincial ones. It has
the exclusive control over the Supplies necessary

---

* Imperial Act, 28 and 29 Vic., cap. 63.

to carry on any sort of Government ; and it has in its hands the power of deciding to whom the Administration of Government will be entrusted. In other words, it has the power of change of Ministry, for no Ministry can carry on a Government, for any length of time, unless supported by a majority in Parliament. The duties and powers of an Administration will be referred to hereafter, under the head of Administrative Government. It is noted for the present, as one of the consequential powers of Parliament. Parliament, by enacting private Bills, such as incorporating companies, or conferring privileges, or in removing restraints, &c., deals largely in Legislation of a Judicial character, which forms the greater bulk of its work, and is of great importance to the country.

In the removal of Judges the Parliament can take action on addresses presented to it for that purpose. Although the appointment of the Judges rests with the Governor in Council the Parliament has a remedy for the removal of incompetent ones.

The privileges, immunities and powers of the two Houses of Parliament must not exceed those enjoyed by the House of Commons in England. If the provision in the Act of 1867 transfers all the law and customs of the Commons in England, the two Houses of the Dominion Parliament are on a far different footing from what Colonial Assemblies in general are. They still are not in the corresponding positions of the two Houses in England.

A very distinguished Colonial lawyer, Chief Justice Morris, remarks of the early Assemblies in North America :

" When any question arises here concerning a Governor in Assembly, many are ready to ask what the King or Parliament of England does on a like occasion, vainly thinking that whatever is done by a King or Parliament is fit to be drawn into example for the place. However extensive that notion may be in America, it is rather to be laughed at than argued with, not but that the wisdom and regularity of a British Parliament are very fit patterns so far as they are imitable by us."

The English Parliament has a law and custom of its own which are not part of the Common Law of England, but are separate and distinct from it. Parliament there stands on its own law. Colonial Assemblies are not on the same footing, they derive their energies from the Crown, and are regulated by charter and usages and by the Common Law of England. Indeed it is laid down broadly that the principle upon which the English Parliament rests its rights, powers and privileges cannot be extended to a Provincial Assembly.*

* Chalmer's Opinions.

CHAPTER VIII

The Governor General, under advice, exercises the power of summoning Parliament, proroguing it when necessary or desirable, and dissolving it, so far as the Commons is concerned, within the period of five years from its commencement. The Senate and Commons are summoned by Proclamation to attend at Ottawa on a certain day, usually in February, " for the despatch of business; to treat, do, act and conclude upon those things which in our said Parliament of Canada, by the Common Council of our said Dominion, may by the favour of God be ordained."

The Parliament is opened by the Governor in person in the Senate Chamber. The Senators being assembled the Speaker commands the Gentleman Usher of the Black Rod to proceed to the Commons and acquaint that House that "it is His Excellency's pleasure that they attend him immediately in this House." The Commons then proceed in a body to the bar of the Senate, and, if at the beginning of a new Parliament, are instructed to choose a Speaker for their House. They then return to their own House, and having chosen a Speaker, are again summoned to the Senate, usually on the following day, and the Speaker is then presented to the Governor-General. The Speaker is the official means of communication between his House and the Governor-General, and between the House and Judges who make returns as to the Election Petitions.

In the Senate the Speaker takes part with the other Senators in debate. They do not address him, though he occupies the Chair in the Senate, but they address the rest of the Senators. Any intemperate or offensive language is dealt with by the Senate, which may censure the delinquent, and may also interfere to prevent quarrels between Senators. They do not vote by "Ayes" and "Noes," but those in favor of the motion are the "Contents," and those opposing it the "Non-Contents." In all unprovided cases the rules, usages and forms of the House of Lords are to be followed.

The Speaker of the Commons is the First Commoner in the Dominion, and has most important duties to perform. He decides on all questions of Order and of Parliamentary Practice, and sees that the Orders of the House are carried out, and is judge of what is improper or unparliamentary. He takes no part in the debates, but has the casting vote in the case of an equality of votes. He preserves order and decorum in the House, and the members address him instead of the other members. He decides questions of order, subject to appeal to the House, and he apprises the House of what is unparliamentary. He has charge of the officers and clerks in attendance on the House, fills vacancies therein, and fixes salaries of new employees. Both Speakers have to do with the Library of Parliament, and during the Session no persons except the Governor-General and the members and officers of both Houses can resort thither unless under authority from one of the Speakers. In all unprovided cases the rules, usages and forms of the English House of Commons are to be followed in the Commons in Canada.

English and French may be used in the debates in both Houses, and the journals of the debates are entered in both languages.

The House ordinarily meets every day at three o'clock, except on Saturdays; and if sufficient members are present to form a quorum, proceeds to the despatch of business. This number, as has been remarked, is fifteen in the Senate and twenty in the Commons, of which number the Speaker in each may be reckoned as one. Certain routine business, such as presenting and receiving petitions, and presenting reports of the different committees in the House, and motions, are taken up every day as they occur, and afterwards the Orders of the Day, which are different every day, are read, and proceeded with. A day or more in the week is usually reserved to the Government, in view of the large amount of business in its hands.

At the beginning of each Parliament, and each of its subsequent sessions, the Governor-

General opens the session with a gracious speech
to both Houses, which is reported to them by
the Speaker of the Senate. This is supposed
to contain the leading points of proposed legislation on the part of the Government. Before
it is reported some Bill is read *pro forma*.
Afterwards the speech is discussed in the House,
and, if carried, a reply presented to the Governor-
General. The legislation of the session is then
taken up.

Every member is privileged to bring in a
motion or Bill; but in the Commons he must
give notice of his intention to bring in a Bill.
When a Bill is brought in the House it is read
simply without discussion. On the second reading the principles of the Bill are discussed.
If not interrupted at this or towards the next
stage, the Bill is committed ; that is, it is taken
into consideration in a committee of the House.
When the House goes into Committee the
Speaker leaves the Chair, and the Mace, which
represents Royal authority, is put under the
table. The House may then appoint any member as Chairman, and the strict rules of debate
observed in Parliament are relaxed. In Committee each clause of the Bill is considered and
voted upon. If the Committee have not time to
get through they ask leave to sit again. When
ready to report, or when the Committee must
rise, the Speaker resumes the Chair, and the
House proceeds to business. If ready, the Bill
is then read a third time. The only parts usu-

ally left for a fourth reading are the preamble and title, which are always the last things considered. The Bill, having gone through these different stages in the House where it originates, is sent to the other House, where it passes through the same stages as to readings.

In case of amendments by one House on a Bill sent from the other, the Senate arranges *conferences* to bring about an agreement. For this purpose each House appoints its own bearers of messages. One of the Clerks of either House may be a bearer from one House to another, and the Master in Chancery, attending the Senate. is received as their messenger to the Commons. Messages may also be brought up by two or more members of the Commons to the Senate. A Committee of either House does not receive a message from the other. The Speaker takes the chair; and the message, after being read at the Bar, is delivered to the Speaker, who reports the same to his House. The answer is sent and received with corresponding formality. If no agreement as to amendment is arrived at, the Bill is lost.

After having been passed by both Houses, it only requires the assent of the Governor-General to make it an Act of Parliament. When a Bill passed by both Houses is presented to His Excellency, he has three courses constitutionally open to him. He may assent to the Bill. in the Queen's name; he may withhold the Queen's assent; or he may reserve the Bill for the signification of the Queen's pleasure. The Queen's assent is seldom withheld : but not unfrequently Bills are reserved for the signification of Her pleasure. The Royal instructions to the Governor-General sometimes set out specifically certain Bills, such as Divorce, &c., which must be reserved.

All Bills, except the Supply Bill, are supposed to come from the Senate to the Crown. The Supply Bill being essentially a Bill of the House of Commons, is assented to specially by the Governor-General, thanking them for affording the funds necessary to carry on the Government of the country. The Crown suggests the supplies ; and probably if the case should arise in this country the Crown would originate a Bill for a general pardon in analogy to British precedent. Beyond this, all measures originate indifferently either in the Senate or Commons. Some Bills are left to be originated in Select Committees, some in Committee of the whole House. The Public Bills affect the whole Dominion—Private Bills affect individuals, companies, or corporations. These latter Bills, before being entertained, require a deposit of $100 in the Senate and $200 in the Commons, and the costs of printing and translating the copies sent in. This is in order to cover the expense of printing, &c., and Private Bills must be advertised in the *Canada Gazette*, the official journal of the Government, for two months before the House opens.

CHAPTER IX

THE Privy Council of Canada, as in England, is assumed to be the past and present advisers of the Crown. Privy Councillors are to aid and advise in the Government of Canada, and are chosen and summoned by the Governor-General to advise and assist him in every way that good Councillors should do. Persons who have been Ministers of the Crown since Confederation, whether in or out of office, are said to be members of the Privy Council, though what is generally understood by the term is the acting Ministry for the time being. This is known here and in England as the Cabinet Council. The remainder of the Privy Councillors who are not supporters of the Ministry take no part in the Government. As they are usually the former Ministers of a defeated Government, they form the leading spirits in the Opposition. They are Privy Councillors without being summoned to the Cabinet Council.

All the Privy Councillors are sworn in as such on accepting office, and are chosen for life; that is, they are liable to be summoned at any time to take part in forming a Government. In order to be a member of the Government a Privy Councillor, if not a Senator, must have a seat in the Commons. An acting Minister must be in either House, but he cannot be a member of both Houses at the same time. A member of the Privy Council may be a member of the Cabinet and yet have no portfolio in the Government; that is, may not be the head of any of the Departments of State, and answerable to the House of Commons or Senate for his share or conduct of the public affairs of the Dominion. The Government as a body is answerable for all acts of its Ministers whether they have portfolios or not.

The Cabinet, or Ministry, is now composed of thirteen members; twelve of these have charge of the different departments into which the work of governing the country is divided, and one is President of the Council, with no very defined duties to perform. The duties of the Ministers having charge of Departments are laid down by Act of Parliament; and they are obliged to report annually to Parliament, as to the matters under their control. This most important part of the management of Public Affairs is called Administrative Government, and will be detailed in the next few chapters.

Besides the individual duties of the Ministers, the Privy Council, as a body, have very important powers and duties. They advise the Governor-General, it may be safely said, upon all his Official Acts, and they, and not he, are responsible for all Parliamentary Enactments, all Proclamations, all Orders in Council, &c.

As advisers of the Crown, they must see not only that the Parliament of Canada keeps within its due limits, but that the Provincial Legislatures do not transgress their Constitutional bounds in legislation or otherwise. They advise the Governor-General of the proper persons to be Lieutenant-Governors of the Province, and suggest his removal when the gravity of the case may require it. They are, in short, responsible for the Legislation passed in Parliament, or permitted, or omitted to be passed ; for the due execution of the laws, whether done under their own supervision in the Department of State or otherwise ; and with them rests the appointment of Judges for the construction and interpretation of the laws, when enacted. In this country they are themselves relieved from any Judicial functions, as there is no such thing as a Judicial Committee of the Privy Council in Canada, as a Court of Appeal. The occasion does not arise for similar duties to the Judicial Committee of the Privy Council in England, as the latter entertains chiefly appeals from the Colonies, which of course Canada could not have. The Judicial Committee of the Privy Council in England determines all matters that can come judicially before the Queen ; and amongst others, decides on all matters of Colonial reference, and is the ultimate resort of a Colonial subject, on an appeal from the laws of his own colony. The Privy Council in Canada can refer certain matters to the Supreme Court at Ottawa, as will be referred to hereafter.

The duties of the Privy Councillors, as defined by their oath of office, are to serve her Majesty truly and faithfully in her Council; to keep secret all matters treated, debated or resolved in the Privy Council from all persons outside of that body : and if the matter refer to any member of the Council concerning his loyalty and fidelity, then it must not be disclosed to that member until the Queen's pleasure be known in that behalf. They must in all things faithfully, honestly and truly declare their mind and opinion to the honor and benefit of her Majesty ; and in , general be vigilant, diligent and circumspect in all their doings touching the Queen's affairs, as good Councillors should do.

These functions of the Privy Council are exercised by the Cabinet Council ; but the oath taken by each Privy Councillor on his accepting office would oblige him to be mindful of these duties during his life-time, his appointment lasting during that period. Complete harmony of action is required among the members of the Government when what are called " Cabinet questions " arise. If any member of the Government fails to agree with the views of the Council on such questions it is his duty to resign. On these questions the Government of the day stands or falls together. Measures initiated by members of the Government are not necessarily measures upon which, if the Ministry are defeated in the Commons, it would be their duty to resign. But if the Ministry make any question, otherwise not a Government measure, to be such, then their defeat on that would give rise to votes of want of confidence, which, if successful, would necessitate a change of Ministry.

The Cabinet Council is, therefore, a fluctuating body, which, besides being the choice of the Crown, is also the approved party of the two Houses of Parliament. The Cabinet, on one side, takes its origin in the two Houses of Parliament, and on the other exists and acts in the Executive. It is well defined as the connecting link between the Legislative and Executive authority.* For, although in theory the Queen is the Executive, the Privy Council or Government is the real Executive. The other is a fiction perpetuated here by statute. but none the less a fiction. The Queen, or Governor-General in Canada, does every thing, it is true, but does it because the Privy Council advise so: and without such advice nothing is done.

The Privy Council is a section of the Houses of Parliament, and yet it rules not only the first estate, but the other two as well. In fact, it is a deputed Committee of Parliament which carries on the Government. Its aim is to please the Senate and Commons. So long as it does that it cannot displease the Crown. Whatever

---

* Bagehot, on The English Constitution.

they advise is done, and presumably is done for
the best, as the people are satisfied, and when
they are, the Crown is satisfied. The Crown has
no choice in reality; it discovers the people's
choice, and then selects him as Leader—as
Prime Minister. He is the double choice, and
our Constitution does not admit of the supposi-
tion that the Crown will choose any one not the
choice of the people. This is not saying but
that the Crown has certain abstract rights; but
these are obsolete and disused in England, and
can have no application here. The Cabinet
Council, in effect, governs the people; and the
people, and the people only, have to say of whom
the Cabinet is to be composed. It is their loss
or gain, and is their choice by right. The Crown
approves without interfering.

CHAPTER X.

HAVING considered the Legislative functions of the Government of Canada, attention will now be directed to its Executive. This is divided into two parts by some writers, viz., Administrative and Judicial Government; but the three duties of Government in making, explaining and enforcing laws will be found to be convenient.

The Executive Government and authority in and over Canada is vested in the Queen. The Government of Canada is carried on by and on behalf of the Queen by a Governor-General aided and assisted by Privy Councillors. What prerogatives of Royalty can be exercised by the Governor-General are not easily ascertained, as was seen in a former chapter. So far in the History of the Dominion it does not appear that he can officially act other than on the advice of his responsible Ministers. When a Ministry resigns, the Crown stands alone with no adviser known to the Constitution. Its first step taken towards the formation of a new Ministry is one taken on advice. A member accepting the position of leader of a new Government is by the theory of the Constitution advising the

Governor-General to that step. The new leader advises by accepting.

Probably the only instance in which a Governor must act on his own independent advice is where he conceives that the Policy of his present advisers is not such as the country would uphold if 'the elective branch were dissolved and the country left to decide the question. This new Ministry would, however, have to shoulder the responsibility of this extraordinary course. It may well happen that a Ministry, even in good faith, would mistake the right course where several are open to it, and then feel itself bound to continue that course. A prudent Governor, superior to party and viewing his country from an elevation higher than his advisers view it, may conclude that the country would not approve of such a course as his Ministry advise him to pursue. The Crown outlives party; to-day one set of advisers are in power, and to morrow they are gone. He remains, and in extraordinary emergencies his timely check may save his country.

This, however, may not happen, with a series of Governors, in the space of a century. His Ministry for the time being, represent the people; and it is more reasonable that he should take their advice than that they take his, and the responsibility of it, at the same time. They cannot avoid the responsibility; and they would be ridiculous and inconsistent in saying the advice was not theirs, but was the Governor's. He is not responsible to the people, but his Ministry is; and it is generally better for the people to have a Governor who will follow his advisers, than to have one looking for advisers. In the ordinary course of events, there could be no hesitancy in preferring the advice of a responsible Ministry to that of an irresponsible official.

The people have decided who is to rule them for a term of years at a time. Their choice may have been unfortunate, but there appears no way of recalling it, unless the Governor fancies he can safely dissolve the House on the strength of what he believes the public sentiment to be. This may sometimes be necessary and expedient; but it is a dangerous experiment, and appears to be contrary to the spirit of the British Constitution in modern times. The Crown is satisfied at the choice the people *have* made in the last election—it does not speculate, as to what choice they will make in the next.

The fact seems to be that some body must take the responsibility of even this official act of the Governor-General, either the outgoing or incoming Ministry as to change of Government. The moment any one accepts the leadership, he tenders advice as to the choice.

In the exercise of the Royal Prerogative of Pardon the British Government for a long time

held out that the exercise of this power vested in
the Governor-General without the advice of his
Ministers; but they amended the instructions to
Lord Dufferin on this point on the able arguments
advanced by the Canadian Minister of Justice,
the Hon. Edward Blake.

Other administrative statutory rights of the
Crown, such as convoking or dissolving Parlia-
ment, appointing Judges, appointing Lieutenant-
Governors, &c., though vested in the Governor-
General are, in reality, done under advice from
responsible Ministers.

II. The Parliament.

The administrative functions of Parliament
have already been referred to. By the defeat of
the acting Administration on a test question they
force them to resign. The Parliament, in case
the Crown refuses to agree with it, can refuse
the Supplies and create a deadlock in public
affairs. It has also the removal of Judges in its
power, on petition made for that purpose.

III. Privy Council Collectively.

The administrative functions of the Privy
Council as a body consist in promulgating Orders
in Council which have the effect of laws, issuing
proclamations, directing enquiries in public
matters, taking action in unforeseen emergencies,
and advising in all matters done officially by the
Governor-General in Council and out of it. The

proceedings of the Privy Council are secret, or supposed to be so, and the Council is presided over by one of their members called the President of the Council. The Governor-General is not often present; on exceptional occasions he presides. The practice was reported to England to be that the questions of State are discussed by the Council and by the First Minister, and reported to the Governor-General.

CHAPTER XI.

ADMINISTRATIVE GOVERNMENT.—MINISTERS' DEPART-
MENTAL DUTIES.

The task of administering the public affairs of Canada is divided into twelve departments, each presided over by a Minister, who makes an annual report to Parliament by command of the Governor-General. If the administration of public affairs is not to the satisfaction of Parliament the task can be handed over to others. No particular place is assigned to the Leader, or Prime Minister. In England the Leader is usually First Lord of the Treasury, but the Departmental work there is not at all similar to what it is in Canada.

Each Minister is paid $7,000 per annum as compensation for his labor. The Ministers in the different Departments at Ottawa are assisted by deputies and assistants, who form the Civil Service of Canada. The following are the Departments as they stand at present, since the Statutes of 1879:

1. The Department of Justice.
2. The Department of Finance.
3. The Department of Agriculture.
4. The Department of the Secretary of State of Canada.
5. The Department of Militia and Defence.
6. The Department of Customs.
7. The Department of Inland Revenue.
8. The Department of the Interior.
9. The Department of Public Works.
10. The Department of Railways and Canals.
11. The Post Office Department.
12. The Department of Marine and Fisheries.

CHAPTER XII.

1. The Department of Justice.

This Department of the Civil Service is presided over by the Minister of Justice for Canada, who is appointed by the Governor-General, by Commission, under the Great Seal, and who holds office during pleasure—that is, so long as the Government, of which he is a member, retains office. The Minister of Justice is by virtue of his office Attorney-General of Canada, and in this regard, he is entrusted with the same powers, and charged with the same duties, which belong to the office of Attorney-General for England, by law, or usage, so far as the same powers and duties are applicable to Canada; and also with such powers and duties as belonged to that office, prior to 1867, in the Province, in order to carry out the provisions of the Confederation Act by the Government of the Dominion.

He is Legal Adviser of the Governor-General, and the Legal Member of the Privy Council. He must see that the Administration of Public Affairs is in accordance with law. He has the superintendence of all matters connected with the Administration of Justice in Canada, that does not fall within the Jurisdiction of the Provinces. He must advise upon the Legislation of the Provinces in case it be in excess of their

powers, and must advise the Crown generally
upon all matters of law referred to him. He
advises the heads of the other Departments upon
all matters of Law connected with their
departments. He settles and approves of all
Instruments issued under the Great Seal of
Canada, has the conduct and regulation of all
litigation for or against the Crown, or any
Public Department, in matters within the
authority and jurisdiction of the Dominion ; and
he may have to advise on other matters referred
to him by the Governor in Council. He has
also the superintendence of Penitentiaries and
the Prison system of the Dominion, and returns
are made to him every year from Penitentiaries,
Gaols, Lunatic Asylums and Reformatories.

The Governor appoints a Deputy of the
Minister of Justice, who is charged with the
performance of these Departmental duties,
under the Minister. He has the control and
management of the officers, clerks and servants
of the Department, who are appointed by the
Governor, and he may have other powers and
duties assigned him by the Governor in Council.

By order in Council, dated in February, 1876,
rules for proceedings in the Supreme Court were
promulgated, and the general practice of the
Court in receiving and hearing appeals was laid
down.

The Minister of Justice is now a member of
the Treasury Board in the room, and stead of
the Receiver-General.

CHAPTER XIII.

ADMINISTRATIVE GOVERNMENT.—(CONTINUED.)

2. THE DEPARTMENT OF FINANCE.

THIS Department of the Civil Service is presided over by the Minister of Finance and Receiver General, appointed and holding office like the Minister of Justice and the other Ministers of the Crown.

This Department has the supervision, control and direction of all matters relating to the Financial Affairs and Public Accounts, Revenue and Expenditure of the Dominion, excepting such of these matters as may be assigned to other departments, as Customs, &c.

The Governor-General appoints a Deputy Minister of Finance, who is Deputy Head of the Department and Secretary of the Treasury Board. Formerly the Auditor General and an officer called the Deputy Inspector General were officers of this Department. A Board called the Treasury Board, consisting of the Minister of Finance, the Minister of Justice, the Minister of Customs, and the Minister of Inland Revenue is a Committee of the Privy Council on all matters mentioned as belonging to this Department. The Board may call the attention of the Council to any of these matters, or the Council may refer any of them to the Board. The Board has power to require from any Public Department, Board or Officer, or other person or party bound by law to furnish the same to the Government, any account, return, statement, document, or information which the Board may think necessary for the due performance of its duties. By the word Revenue in this Department is meant Revenue of the Dominion of Canada and all branches thereof, and all public moneys, whether arising from duties of Customs or other duties, or from the Post Office, or from tolls on Canals, Railways or other public works, or from penalties or forfeitures, or rents or dues, or other source whatsoever, and whether the money belongs to or is collected by the Dominion in trust for any Province or for Great Britain. The Governor in Council determines what officers are necessary in the collection of the Revenue, and divides up Canada into posts and districts for Revenue purposes, and makes all necessary regulations for payment and accounting for the Revenue. No money is paid out of the Public Chest unless by cheque on some bank upon the warrant of the Governor in Council, signed by the Receiver General and countersigned by the Minister of Finance, or their respective Deputies.

The Governor appoints a Board of Audit, whose duty it is to report on any accounts laid before it. This Board consists of the Deputy Postmaster-General, the Commissioner of Customs, the Commissioner of Inland Revenue, the

Deputy Minister of Finance, the Deputy of the Minister of Public Works, the Deputy of the Minister of Militia, the Deputy of the Minister of Marine and Fisheries, and an Auditor-General, appointed by the Governor, who is Chairman of the Board. This Board examines into public accounts submitted to them, and reports to the Minister of Finance, and no decision of the Board is binding until approved of by him. The Board prepares and submits to the Minister of Finance the public accounts to be annually laid before Parliament for the financial year. The financial year begins on the 30th of June in each year. This Board has power to examine persons on oath, to obtain writs of summons, issue commissions, and to take evidence when necessary.

This Department has to deal with banks issuing Dominion notes in place of their own, and also with the issue of Dominion notes, and with the currency generally.

The Minister of Finance is now Receiver-General, and has all the powers and duties which the Receiver-General was charged with.

For the more complete examination of the public accounts, and for the reporting thereon, the Governor General may, under the Great Seal, appoint an Auditor General of Canada, who holds office till removed by the Governor-General on the address of the Senate and Commons. He issues all cheques under the Parliamentary appropriation, and unless in these cases no cheque of the Finance Minister shall issue unless upon his certificate. He certifies and reports as to the public accounts presented to Parliament by the Minister.

The Deputy of the Minister shall keep the accounts with the Financial Agents of the Dominion in England and with the banks paying or receiving public money, and accounts of money paid for interest on Canadian stock, debentures or other securities. He shall countersign all debentures and keep a debenture book, an interest book respecting them, and an appropriation book, and shall keep the public accounts of the Dominion, and has control and direction of its financial affairs, public accounts, revenue and expenditure under the Minister. He prepares and submits to the Ministers the public accounts to be laid before Parliament. The manner of dealing with this most important part of the public affairs in the Finance Department is too complicated to give even a general idea of its workings within a small space. The reader must be referred to Public Accounts Audit Act, 1878, and its amendments.

CHAPTER XIV.

3. THE DEPARTMENT OF AGRICULTURE.

THIS Department is presided over by the Minister of Agriculture, who, with a Deputy Minister, has charge of the management and direction of the Department.

The duties and powers of the Minister of Agriculture, extend to the execution of the laws enacted by the Parliament of Canada, and of the orders of the Governor-General in Council relating to the following subjects, which are controlled and directed by the Department:

1. Agriculture.
2. Immigration and Emigration.
3. Public Health and Quarantine.
4. The Marine and Emigrant Hospital at Quebec.
5. Arts and Manufactures.
6. The Census, Statistics and the Registration of Statistics.
7. Patents of Invention.
8. Copyright.
9. Industrial Designs and Trade Marks.

Any of these powers and duties may be assigned to other members of the Privy Council by the Governor in Council, and the same power may also assign additional duties to the Minister of Agriculture than those above enumerated. The Minister is bound to make his Annual Report to both Houses of Parliament within twenty days after the commencement of the Session.

Each of the Provinces has power to Legislate in relation to Agriculture in its respective Province, and also in relation to Immigration into such Province. The Dominion has power to Legislate, in relation to these same subjects, in all or any of the Provinces; and the Provincial law takes effect so long and as far only as it is not repugnant to any Act of the Parliament of Canada. These two subjects of Agriculture and Immigration into the Provinces are the only subjects in which Canada and the Provinces have concurrent Jurisdiction. Canada maintains Emigration Offices in Great Britain and in Canada; and arrangements are entered into by which the Dominion and Provincial Governments assist each other in this particular; and conferences of the delegates of both Governments are convened from time to time in the Office of this Department. Minute statutory Regulations are made in regard to Immigrants, Quarantine, &c.; and the Governor in Council is empowered to make regulations to carry out the Quarantine Act, or prohibit the landing of vicious immigrants, &c.

The Minister of Agriculture keeps a register of Copyrights, in which proprietors of literary, scientific and artistic works or compositions may register the same under the Copyright Act of 1875. The Minister has power to make rules and regulations and prescribe forms for this purpose. The term of copyright is for twenty-eight years, and may, under certain circumstances, be renewed for fourteen years after the expiration of that time. Two copies of the work are deposited in this Office, one of which is forwarded to the Library of Parliament. The notice of obtaining a copyright must appear in the work itself in a prescribed form. The rules and regulations are laid down by an order of the Privy Council dated 7th December, 1875. The regulations as to Trade-marks and Designs were laid down by Statute in 1879.

The Minister of Agriculture receives returns as to criminal statistics every year up to the 30th September, from the proper officers of the courts administering criminal justice, and from Wardens and Sheriffs and Justices of the Peace, and records of the same are kept in his Department. He receives also such returns as to the exercise of the prerogative of mercy as are furnished by the Secretary of State. These statistics and returns are abstracted and printed yearly.

A Census shall be taken in 1881, and in every tenth year thereafter, at the beginning of each such year. The details of the Census shall be directed by the Governor in Council; and this Department shall prepare all forms and instructions necessary for that purpose, and examine into the returns and records, and lay before

Parliament such abstracts and tabular returns shewing the results of the Census as accurately and fully as possible.

The Minister of Agriculture is, under the approval of the Governor in Council, from time to time to collect, abstract, tabulate and publish the Vital, Agricultural, Commercial, Criminal and other statistics of the country ; and has all the necessary powers to provide himself with all proper officers and assistants for that purpose. Regulations as to Contageous Diseases in Cattle issue from this Department by order of the Governor in Council.

CHAPTER XV

4. The Department of the Secretary of State of Canada.

The Department is presided over by the Secretary of State of Canada, and managed under his direction. The Governor-General may also appoint an " Under Secretary of State" and other necessary officers.

The duty of this Minister is to have charge of the State Correspondence, to keep all State Records and papers not specially transferred to other Departments, and to perform such other duties as may be assigned him. He is the Registrar General of Canada, and as such registers all Instruments of Summons, Commissions, Letters Patent, Writs, and other Instruments issued under the Great Seal ; and the Under Secretary of State, as Deputy Registrar General of Canada, may sign and certify the registration of all instruments and documents required to be registered, and may issue certified or authenticated copies of these or any records in the office which may be so required. He has also control of the tariff of fees in the application of Letters-patent, and it is through his Department that these issue.

The office of Superintendent of Indian Affairs was formerly entrusted to this Minister ; and he had control and management of the lands and property of the Indians in Canada ; but now this is assigned to the Minister of the Interior.

The Secretary of State had formerly charge of the North-West Mounted Police. This is now transferred to the Minister of the Interior.

All powers and duties vested in the Commissioner of Crown Lands, with respect to Ordinance or Admiralty Lands in the late Province of Canada, are transferred and vested in the Secretary of State, and are to be exercised and performed by him. He has also control and management of all Dominion Crown Lands not specially under the control of the Public Works Department.

The Secretary of State reports annually to Parliament within ten days after its commencement.

The Secretary of State has charge of the State correspondence with the Provinces, as there is now no Secretary of State for the Provinces. He has charge of supplying the stationery required by the several Departments of the Government, and has charge of the Stationery Department, and the Queen's Printer is an officer of this Department.

The Queen's Printer for Canada is appointed by commission under the Great Seal, and holds office during pleasure. He prints and publishes, under the authority of the Governor in Council, the Official Gazette of the Dominion, known as the *Canada Gazette.* All the requisite departmental and other reports, forms, documents and other papers, all State Proclamations, and all official notices, advertisements and documents relating to the Dominion of Canada and under the control of Parliament, and requiring publication, must be published in the *Canada Gazette*, unless some other mode of publication is required by law.

CHAPTER XVI.

5. The Department of Marine and Fisheries.

The Minister of Marine and Fisheries has the management and direction of this Public Department under his control. His Deputy directs and oversees the other officers and servants of the Department, and has general control of its business in the absence of the Minister.

The following are the matters within the control of this Department, under any existing laws in reference thereto :

1. Sea, Coast and Inland Fisheries, and the management regulation and protection thereof, and anything relating thereto ;

2. Trinity Houses and Trinity Boards, Pilots and Pilotage, and Decayed Pilots' Funds ;

3. Beacons, Buoys, Lights, Light-Houses, and their maintenance ;

4. Harbors, Ports, Piers and Wharves, Steamers and Vessels belonging to the Government of Canada, except Gunboats or other Vessels of War ;

5. Harbor Commissioners and Harbor Masters ;

6. Classification of Vessels, and examination and granting of Certificates of Masters and Mates, and others in the Merchant service ;

7. Shipping Masters and Shipping Officers ;

8. Inspection of Steamboats and boards of Steamboat inspection ;

9. Enquiries into causes of Shipwrecks ;

10. Establishment, regulation and maintenance of Marine and Seamen Hospitals and care of distressed seamen, and generally such matters as refer to the Marine and Navigation of Canada.

Orders in Council regulate the close seasons for fish in the different Provinces, and are made on the recommendation of the Minister of this Department.

The Governor in Council may at any time, by Proclamation, transfer from this Department to the Department of Public Works the construction and repair of Light Houses.

CHAPTER XVII.

ADMINISTRATIVE GOVERNMENT.—(Continued.)

6. Department of Militia and Defence.

The Minister of Militia and Defence is charged with and responsible for the administration of Militia Affairs, including all matters involving expenditure, and of the fortifications, gunboats, ordnance, ammunition, arms, armories, stores, munitions, and habiliments of war belonging to Canada. He has also the initiative in all Militia Affairs involving the expenditure of money. The Governor in Council may appoint a Deputy to this Minister, and such other officers as may be necessary, and prescribe their duties.

The Command-in-Chief of the Land and Naval Militia, and of all Naval and Military forces of and in Canada, is vested in the Queen, and shall be exercised and administered by Her Majesty personally, or by the Governor-General as Her representative.

The Militia consists of all the male inhabitants over eighteen years of age and under sixty, not exempted or disqualified by law, and being British subjects by birth or naturalization. There are four classes of Militia, as follows :

1. 18 and over 18, and under 30 years, who are unmarried or widowers without children. These will be called upon to serve first.

2. Those of 30 and upwards, but under 45, unmarried, or widowers, without children. These will be called after the first class.

3. Those of 18 and upwards, but under 45, who are married, or widowers, with children. These will, are next liable to be called.

4. Those of 46 and upwards, but under 60. These are not called until the others are serving.

Her Majesty may, however, in the case of a general rising, or rebellion, require all the male inhabitants of the Dominion, capable of bearing arms, to serve in the Militia.

The Militia is divided into the Active and Reserve Militia.

1. The *Active* consists of three divisions :

(*a.*) The Volunteers, who are composed of corps, raised by enlistment, who serve for three years, in time of peace.

(*b.*) The regulars are composed of men who voluntarily enlist to serve therein, or of men balloted to serve or of men who voluntarily enlist to serve with the balloted men, and of men balloted to serve.

(*c.*) The Marines are composed of seamen sailors, and persons whose usual occupation is upon any steamer, or sailing craft, navigating the waters of the Dominion. The term of service of the Marines and Regulars is two years.

2. The *Reserve* Militia consists of the whole of the men not serving in the Active Militia of the time being.

Canada is divided into twelve Military Districts :

Ontario 4
Quebec 3
Nova Scotia 1
New Brunswick 1
Manitoba 1
British Columbia.. 1
Prince Edward Island 1

Schools of Instruction are established in garrison towns in Canada ; and the staff of Instructors, under the superintendence of a military officer called a Commandant, is appointed by the Governor in Council. The regulations for admission, &c., are laid down by Order in Council.

The Department of Militia and Defence pays those on the pension list. and enquires who are entitled to pensions.

Certain lands in Canada used for military defence, or under the control of the Ordnance Department, are vested in the Secretary of State for War in England, who can dispose of the same or purchase new lands for military purposes.

As regards the Naval defence of the Province, all the lands and other real property, such as docks, dock-yards. arsenals, piers, wharves, quays, &c., vest in the Commissioner of the Admiralty, or Lord High Admiral of England, with power to dispose of the same, and other powers, similar to the Secretary of State for War as to the land defence.

CHAPTER XVIII.

7. The Department of Customs.

The Department of Customs is presided over by the Minister of Customs appointed under the Great Seal, and holding office during pleasure. The Governor-General appoints a Commissioner of Customs, and an Assistant Commissioner of Customs. These have certain powers and perform certain duties assigned them by the Governor-General, or by the Minister of Customs.

This Department has control and management:

1. Of the collection of the duties of Customs and of matters incident thereto, and of the officers and servants employed in that service.

2. Of the Collection of Tolls on the Public Canals, and of matters incident thereto, and of the officers and persons employed in that service, subject to certain Acts, Customs and the Revenue and public accounts and accountants.

The Governor-General may appoint a Board of Examiners for all employees in this department, and these may classify the persons employed, and grant certificates accordingly.

The Minister of Customs reports annually to Parliament on the transactions and affairs of his Department within 15 days after Parliament opens.

CHAPTER XIX

8. THE DEPARTMENT OF INLAND REVENUE.

THIS Department is presided over by the Minister of Inland Revenue, who is assisted by a Commissioner of Inland Revenue and an Assistant Commissioner, called also Inspector of the Department, in performing such duties as are assigned to them by the Governor-General or by the Minister in charge.

This Department has the control and management—

1. Of the collection of all duties of Excise;
2. Of the collection of Stamp Duties and the preparation and issue of stamps and stamped paper, except postage stamps;
3. Of Internal Taxes;
4. Of Standard Weights and Measures;
5. The administration of the laws affecting the culling and measurement of timber, masts, spars, deals and staves, and other articles of a like nature, and the collection of slidage and boomage dues;
6. The collection of Bridge and Ferry tolls and rents;

Subject always to the provisions of the Acts relating to the said subjects and matters connected therewith.

The regulations as to balances, and weighing machines are laid down by order of the Privy Council, dated 10th July, 1877. Under a previous order Canada was divided into ten districts, under the Act respecting Weights and

Measures ; four for Ontario ; two for Quebec ; and one for the other Provinces, except Prince Edward Island. In this office are regulations for the inspection, verification and testing of gas, and for analyzing food, under the Acts to prevent the adulteration of food. The weights and measures Act of 1879 provides for uniformity of weights and measures, and prescribes standards therefor as deposited in this Department.

The Governor-General may appoint officers and other persons to carry out all acts relating to the Department of Inland Revenue, or any orders in Council, or regulations made thereunder. A Board of Examiners may be constituted in this Department, as in that of Customs.

The Minister reports annually to Parliament, within fifteen days after the House opens.

CHAPTER XX.

9. The Department of the Interior.

This Department of the Civil Service is presided over by the Minister of the Interior. He has the control and management of the affairs of the North-West Territories. He is the Superintendent General of Indian Affairs, and has the control and management of their lands and property in Canada. He has also the control and management of all Crown lands, being the property of the Dominion, including those known as Ordnance and Admiralty lands, and all other Public Lands not specially under the control of the Public Works, or of that of Militia and Defence (and excepting also Marine Hospitals and Light Houses, and land connected therewith, and St. Paul's, Stable and Portage Islands). He is substituted for the former Commissioner of Crown Lands as regards Ordnance and Admiralty lands transferred to the late Province of Canada, and lying in Ontario and Quebec.

He takes the place of the Secretary of State in the "Dominion Lands Act of 1872," and has all the powers, attributes, functions, restrictions and duties necessary to the enforcement of the provisions of that Act.

There is a Deputy Minister to this Department who has charge, under the Minister, of the performance of the Departmental duties, and the control and management of the officers, agents, clerks and servants in the Department. The Geological Survey of Canada was attached to this Department.

The Indian Act of 1876 amends and consolidates the law relating to Indians. It defines who they are, what lands they hold and are entitled to, the protection the law affords them, and the disabilities they labor under. The Governor in Council may, however, exempt Indians from any portion of the operations of the Act.

The law relating to the Administration and Management of the Dominion lands is amended and consolidated by an Act passed in 1879 (cap. 31); and these are under the control of the Minister of the Interior in a branch of this Department called " The Dominion Lands Office." This Act provides for the survey and disposal of these lands, regulations as to homesteads, mining and coal fields, timber lands, and licenses thereon, and for the issue of Patents to these lands.

The Minister of this Department has charge of the North-West Mounted Police.

CHAPTER XXI.

10. Post Office Department.

There is at the seat of Government, with the other Public Departments, a Post Office Department, for the superintendence and management of the Postal Service of Canada, under the direction of a Postmaster-General.

He is appointed, like the other Ministers, by Commission under the Great Seal, and holds office, as they do, during pleasure.

He has power to appoint Postmasters having permanent salaries in towns and cities.

He may also subject to the Acts in force :

1. Establish and close Post Offices, and Post routes, and
2. Appoint and suspend Postmasters, and other officers, and servants.
3. Make mail contracts, or other business as to the Post Office, and regulate what is mailable matter, as to size and weight, and prohibit dangerous or improper, or other articles being sent; and establish rates, unless others laid down in Parliament therefor in Canada, and arrange for these outside Canada.
4. Prepare stamps, stamped envelopes, post cards, wrappers, &c., and provide for the sale of the same, and establish a Money Order system, and make necessary regulations as to registration.
5. Establish street letter or pillar boxes, and generally make such regulations as he deems necessary for the due and effective working of his Department.

A Deputy Postmaster-General is appointed by the Governor in Council, who has control of the Department, under the Minister.

The rates of postage on letters, newspapers and periodical publications, and what is called book and parcel post, are laid down by Statute, and the Postmaster-General has no power over these.

The "General Post Union," formed under a treaty taking effect on the 1st of July, 1875, regulates the understanding had between Great Britain and Germany, Austro Hungary, Belgium, Denmark, Egypt, Spain, the United States of America, France, Greece, Italy, Luxembourg, Norway, the Netherlands, Portugal, Roumania, Russia, Servia, Sweden, Switzerland and Turkey.

Postal arrangements and a Money Order system are arranged between Canada and the United States.

The Postmaster General has the sole and exclusive privilege of sending and delivering letters in Canada; and any person who infringes upon this privilege, except as provided, is liable to a penalty of at least $20 for every letter delivered, or found in his possession. The exceptions provided are, letters sent by a private friend, or by a messenger sent on purpose, on private affairs of the sender, or receiver, or sent by a private vessel to a place out of Canada, or letters brought into Canada, and immediately posted; or letters sent with goods, but without pay or return and commissions, or other papers, issuing out of a Court of Justice.

The Postmaster-General reports very fully to Parliament on the Finances, Receipts and Expenditure of his Department; what has been paid for mail transport, salaries of persons employed, incidental expenses, dead and lost letters, the transactions of the money order offices, the losses and costs under this system, and the transactions of the Post Office Savings Bank.

This Report is presented to the House within ten days after the opening of the Session.

CHAPTER XXII.

DEPARTMENT OF PUBLIC WORKS.

PRIOR to the 20th of May, 1879, the Department of Public Works was presided over by one Minister appointed in the usual way. On that day, by Proclamation, it was divided into two departments, to be presided over and managed by two members of the Administration, who are designated as the Minister of Railways and Canals, and the Minister of Public Works.

II. DEPARTMENT OF RAILWAYS AND CANALS.

The Minister in charge of this Department has the management and direction of all Railways, and works and property appertaining or incident thereto, which immediately before the proclamation mentioned were under the management and direction of the Department of Public Works, to the same extent and under the same provisions as they were formerly managed. Each of the two Ministers succeeds to all the powers and duties before vested in the Minister of Public Works, so far as respects the works under their respective charge. In case any doubt arise as to which of them any particular branch of the Public Works belongs, it shall be decided by order of the Governor in Council ; and he may make order assigning any of the officers and employees of the present Department to either of the newly constituted Departments, or direct them to act in both.

The Governor in Council may appoint as chief officer of the Department a Deputy Minister of Railways and Canals, a Secretary, one or more Chief Engineers, a chief Architect, and other necessary officers.

The Deputy has charge of the Department under the Minister, directs the other officers and, has general control of the business of the Department, and may be assigned other duties by the Governor in Council.

The Secretary keeps account of the moneys appropriated for and expended on each Public Work and Building under the management of the Department, keeps accounts with contractors, looks after contracts to see that they are correctly drawn up and executed, prepares certificates, reports, &c.

The Chief Engineer and Architects prepare maps, plans and estimates, and report to the Minister thereon.

The Legislation relating to Railways generally will be found amended and consolidated in chap. 9, 42 Victoria (1879).

12. The Department of Public Works.

The Minister of Public Works presides over this Department, has charge of all Public Works of the Dominion, except the Railways and

Canals, assigned to the Minister of Railways and Canals under the Act of 1879.

He has control of :

1. Works for the Improvement of the Navigation of any water, such as Locks, Dams, Hydraulic Works, Harbour Piers, &c., and Works for facilitating the transmission of timber, such as slides, dams, piers, booms, and other work, except those appertaining or belonging to Canals, or being incident thereto.

2. Roads and bridges, public buildings, vessels, dredges, scows, tools, implements and machinery, for the improvement of navigation, not belonging to canals.

3. The Provincial steamers.

4. All other property (except that managed in the Department of Railways and Canals) heretofore acquired, constructed, repaired, maintained, or improved at the expense of the late Province of Canada, or of New Brunswick and Nova Scotia, or hereafter to be acquired by Canada.

5. Such portions of Ordnance Property transferred to the late Provincial Government of Canada by the Imperial Government, and afterwards placed under this Department.

But any public works or property which were or will be transferred to any of the Provinces mentioned, or leased or sold to Municipalities, incorporations, or other parties, are not within this Department; nor are any public works, roads, bridges, harbors, or property which were abandoned by proclamation to the control of the Municipal or Local authorities.

The Governor-General may, by proclamation, declare any other works, roads, bridges, harbors, slides, light-houses, or buildings purchased or

8

constructed at the public expense, and not assigned to the Provinces, to be under the management of this Department.

All land, streams, water courses, and property acquired for the use of the Public Works, are vested in Her Majesty; and the Minister may take possession and acquire lands necessary for the Public Service in Her name. The price and other conditions are regulated under Arbitration, from which, in cases over $500, an appeal lies to the Exchequer Court of Canada.

Any work for or connected with the Public Defence may, by order in Council, be declared within the management of this Department, saving the rights of the Secretary of State for War as to Imperial interests.

CHAPTER XXIII.

THE expenses of the Public Service of Canada are paid out of what is called the Consolidated Revenue Fund. This fund took its origin from those Duties and Revenues of the late Provinces of Canada, Nova Scotia, and New Brunswick, except such portions as were reserved at the Union in 1867 to the Provinces, or are raised by the Provinces themselves. It is composed of all stocks, cash, bankers' balances and securities; all lands, mines, minerals and royalties; and any sums due or payable thereon which then belonged to the Provinces.

Also the following Public Works :

1. Canals, with Lands and Water Power connected therewith.
2. Public Harbours.
3. Lighthouses and Piers, and Sable Island.
4. Steamboats, Dredges, and Public Vessels.
5. Rivers and Lake Improvements.
6. Railways and Railway Stocks, Mortgages, and other Debts due by Railway Companies.
7. Military Roads.
8. Custom Houses, Post Offices, and all other Public Buildings, except such as the Government of Canada appropriate for the Use of the Provincial Legislatures and Governments.
9. Property transferred by the Imperial Government, and known as Ordnance Property.

10. Armouries, Drill Sheds, Military Clothing, and Munitions of War, and Lands set apart for general Public Purposes.

Beyond this the Provinces retained all their respective Public Property—Canada reserving merely the right to assume any lands or Public Property required for fortifications or defence. In return for this Canada became liable for the debts and liabilities of each of these Provinces at the Union, which were reduced by such stock, cash, bankers, balances, and securities for money as the Provinces had at the time. Canada gave up to Ontario and Quebec conjointly the following properties belonging to the late Province of Canada :

Upper Canada Building Fund.
Lunatic Asylums.
Normal Schools.
Court Houses in
Aylmer,
Montreal, } Lower Canada.
Kamouraska,
Law Society, Upper Canada.
Montreal Turnpike Trust.
University Permanent Fund.
Royal Institution.
Consolidated Municipal Loan Fund, Upper Canada.
Consolidated Municipal Loan Fund, Lower Canada.
Agricultural Society, Upper Canada.
Lower Canada Legislative Grant.
Quebec Fire Loan.
Temiscouata Advance Account.
Quebec Turnpike Trust.
Education, East.
Building and Jury Fund, Lower Canada.
Municipalities Fund.
Lower Canada Superior Education Income Fund.

Although Canada assumed the indebtedness of the Provinces, it was settled at a certain sum, or

if beyond, the Provinces were to pay Canada
interest on the excess at 5 per centum per
annum.

These sums were as follows :

Ontario and Quebec, liable to Canada, if their debt
was over.............................. $62,500,000 00
Nova Scotia........................... 8,000,000 00
New Brunswick........................ 7,000,000 00

If the debts of the latter two Provinces were
not up to their respective amounts, they were to
get the same rate of interest in half yearly payments in advance on the difference.

Canada was to pay towards the expenses of
the Provincial Governments the following sums :

Ontario.............................. $80,000
Quebec 70,000
Nova Scotia......................... 60,000
New Brunswick 50,000

Besides, an annual grant determinable on the
population.

This was the basis of the Consolidated Revenue Fund of Canada in 1867 ; and the balance
of the Duties and Revenues not appropriated
were, along with all Duties and Revenues raised
in accordance with special Provincial powers,
formed into Provincial funds called the Consolidated Revenue Fund of the Province.

These funds are each year augmented in
various ways. In the Dominion Government,
large sums are paid in from the Customs,
Revenue and Public Land Departments, by
means of tariffs, excise, or other duties, by the

sale of lands, by fees from the Post Office Department, and from the various other Departments of State. If the receipts from these sources are in advance of the amount asked for in the Supply Bill, which sets out of the expenditure of the country for the fiscal year, then there is no necessity of direct taxation, or specific grants by Parliament. The Ways and Means used for raising the Supplies forms the Budget of the year ; and when it is considered that in Canada the supplies voted by Parliament usually run a great many million of dollars annually, as the expenses of the Government from July to July, the task which the Minister has in making a satisfactory Budget Speech is not at all an easy one.

The first change in the Consolidated Revenue Fund of Canada is the costs, charges and expenses incident to its collection, management and receipt. The interest on the Public Provincial debts is the second ; and the third is the Governor-General's salary, fixed at £10,000 sterling, or such other sum as the Parliament of Canada may determine. After these payments are made the balance is appropriated to the Public Service of Canada, with no particular order of preference.

The Governor-General in Council, unless Parliament otherwise directs, orders the form and manner of all payments or discharge of liabilities, under the Act of 1867, in regard to Canada and its Provinces in these matters.

CHAPTER XXIV

IT is not easy to define, in a few words, the exact position of the Provinces comprising the Dominion of Canada. In 1867 three existing Provinces desired to be federally united into one Dominion; and they were so united, and formed thereafter Canada. The three Provinces were then lost sight of, and in their stead Canada appeared; and Canada was immediately afterwards divided up into four Provinces. The late Province of Canada, with Nova Scotia and New Brunswick, was constitutionally wiped out of existence; and these portions of the British possessions—these Colonies—were to be thereafter known under a new name collectively, and with new Constitutions. Had the new Political division one Legislature only for all purposes, the difficulty of defining our new situation would be comparatively easy. But the difficulty of legislating for all parts of the new Dominion was deemed by the framers of its Constitution so great that one central Parliament could not satisfactorily accomplish that task. Accordingly, in almost the very next section of the Act of 1867 uniting the three Provinces into Canada, we find it declared that Canada shall be divided into four Provinces, just as these possessions were before the Union Act of 1840 ; and then exclusive powers of legislation are given to the Provinces. The reader will remember that the three Provinces, Canada, Nova Scotia and New Brunswick, were one, might say four, even after 1840 and up to 1867, as the Union Act, though it united Upper and Lower Canada into one Province, recognized their separate existence. The old Provinces retained their geographical boundaries, but lost almost everything else. They merged in the Dominion and were re-created in another set of names—Ontario, Quebec, Nova Scotia and New Brunswick.

There is a great difference, therefore, between the present and past position of these Provinces. Formerly they were Colonies of the Empire, and possessed Governors or Lieutenant-Governors, who were the immediate representatives of the Crown in their Provinces. Now their chief Executive officers are members of the Colonial Administration staff, and are but Lieutenants of the Governor-General of Canada ; and the Provinces are no longer Colonies, but Provinces of a Colony. Under the former Constitution they had, subject to Imperial authority, the right to make laws for the peace, order and good government of their Provinces ; now their Legislative power is limited to a prescribed set of subjects ; and though they are supreme within these Constitutional limits, it seems that they cannot go beyond them. Whether wisely or not, they surrendered a large portion of their rights to the Federal Government at Ottawa to be there determined upon. Any attempted assumption of authority beyond these subjects, if not vetoed by the Governor-General, is liable to be declared unconstitutional by the Provincial or by the Dominion Courts.

Besides these important matters of substance, it is said—whether that be important or not—that they have lost some matters of form. In the present Constitution one PARLIAMENT is given to Canada; to the Provinces of Canada are given Legislatures without being styled Parliaments.

Whether any British possession in America ever had a Parliament before the Dominion of Canada got one, is a question not to be discussed here. No Plantation or Colony ever received it in so many words, although it was certainly assumed to be reproduced under the Constitutions of 1791 and 1840 in the Canadas. If a Legislature has all the deliberative powers necessary, it is not much to discuss, except as a side issue, whether it be a Parliament or not.

Again, it is said that the Lieutenant-Governors, being deputies of the Governor General, and not of the Queen, have no power to give the Queen's sanction to any Act of the Legislature. They assent on behalf of the Governor-General.* They have not the power to do so under the written Constitution; and there is certainly something

* Per Draper, C. J., *in re* Goodhue, 19 Grant.

anomalous in the case of the Governor-General, the Queen's Deputy, disallowing an Act passed in the Provincial Legislatures by the Queen's Most Excellent Majesty. An objection was formerly raised in the American colonies in the corresponding case of a Governor-General who was unquestionably the Royal Representative, but it was over-ruled. On the matter being referred to England an opinion was given in these words:

"I have heard objections drawn from the style of this Act. 'It is enacted by the King's Most Excellent Majesty,' &c., but I think this objection of little weight. The King is here named in his Royal and Politic capacity, which at the time of making the Act it was to this purpose residing in his Governor, who there enjoyed and exercised the functions of it in this province, and the personal assent was not necessary to the Act." *

Under the strict reading of the Constitution, and in view of the authorities, it would seem, however, that the use of the Queen's name is unauthorized in Acts in the Local Legislatures.

"The Queen" says Mr. Justice Gwynne, forms no part of the Provincial Legislatures, as she does of the Dominion Parliament. * * The use of Her Majesty's name by these Provincial Authorities is by the Act confined to the summoning and calling together the Legislatures ; and singularly as it seems, this is by the 82nd Section, rather by accident I apprehend, than design, confined to the Lieutenant-Governors of Ontario and Quebec.

---

* Chalmer's Opinions.

By the 91st Section it is declared that the Acts of the Dominion Parliament shall be made by the Queen, by and with the advice of the Senate and Commons, treating the Queen herself as an integral part of the Parliament ; whilst the 92nd Section enacts that the ·· Legislatures" of the respective Provinces, that is, the Lieutenant-Governor and the Legislative Assembly in Provinces having but one House, and the Lieutenant-Governor and the Legislative Council and Assembly in Provinces having two Houses, shall make laws in relation to matters coming within certain enumerated classes of subjects, to which their jurisdiction is limited. Nothing can be plainer, as it seems to me, than that the several Provinces are subordinate to the Dominion Government ; and that the Queen is no party to the laws made by those Local Legis·latures, and that no Act of any such Legislatures can in any manner impair or affect Her Majesty's right to the exclusive exercise of all Her prerogative powers, which she continues to enjoy untrammeled, except in so far as we are obliged to hold that, by the express terms of the British North America Act, or by irresistible inference from what is there expressed, she has by that Act consented to be divested of any part of such prerogative."*

* Lenoir *vs.* Ritchie, in the Supreme Court, not yet reported. The foregoing parts of this chapter were in type before this judgment of Mr. Justice Gwynne, appeared in the *Canada Law Journal.*

CHAPTER XXV.

THE LIEUTENANT GOVERNORS.

UNDER the Federal system of Government in Canada the chief executive officers in the Province are now members of the Civil Service of Canada, and not as formerly, members of the Civil Service of England. They are neither appointed nor removed by the Crown, but by the Governor-General of Canada, as will be referred to presently. They are Local not Imperial officers. The Lieutenant-Governor is head of the Legislature, or rather the Legislature is composed of a Lieutanant-Governor and a House of Assembly, either with or without a Legislative Council. He is essential to the Legislature, and is Chief of the Executive in the Provinces. His assent to all Bills in behalf of the Governor-General is necessary before they become law; and he has a negative voice, probably the same as the Crown, in all Legislative Acts. He is the Chief Executive Officer in the Provinces, as has been said; but the Executive Authority of and over the Province is not vested in him. It is, no doubt, vested in the Queen, in whom "the Executive Government and authority of and over Canada is continued and vested."

The Governor in Council appoints a Lieutenant-Governor for each Province, and determines

the length of his official existence, which is
usually five years. He cannot be removed
within that period without cause assigned. This
cause is to be communicated to him in writing
within one month after the order for his removal
is made ; and shall be communicated by message
to the Senate and to the House of Commons
within one-week thereafter, if the Parliament is
then sitting; and if not, then within one week
after the commencement of the next session of
the Parliament. The Senate and Commons
must be the judges as to sufficiency of the cause
alleged. It appears that it is sufficient for the
Ministry at Ottawa that Parliament has passed
a censure on his conduct. Whenever it is felt
by the Dominion Government that it is for the
public interest he should be displaced, then he
is and ought to be removable. He has no vested
right to his office for the full term ; nor does he
hold office during good behavior, like our Judges.*
He is answerable to the Governor in Council,
just the same as that officer is answerable to the
Imperial Government ; and the Administration
of the day must take the responsibility of his
removal precisely the same as of any other
Administrative act. The cause may be insufficient or unreasonable ; but when the cause is
assigned for his removal, and the Parliament

* Sir John A. Macdonald's memorandum to the Governor General in
the Letellier case.

expresses itself thereon, the Constitutional powers of the Governor-General to dismiss a Lieutenant-Governor of the Provinces cannot be questioned.

So far as to appointment and removal.

In order to give some definite limits, probably to the powers, authorities and functions of a Lieutenant-Governor, a clause was enacted as to these officials in Ontario and Quebec almost identical with that defining the powers of the Governor-General himself, which has been referred to heretofore. The present Lieutenant-Governors of Ontario and Quebec have, therefore, such powers, authorities and functions as continue in existence now, or are capable of being exercised under our altered circumstances as our former Governors or Lieutenant Governors had. They are not the Queen's deputies or representatives—they are not appointed by or recalled by Her. The weight of authority is in favour of saying that no prerogative rights of the Crown vest in them, except such as are conferred by the Act of 1867, and that they have no right to deal with matters of Prerogative. The effect of Earl Kimberley's reply to the Dominion Government in the Queen's Counsel case, 1872, would indicate that the powers of a Lieutenant-Governor since 1867 are not so great as they were formerly. He says :

"The Governor-General has now power as Her Majesty's representative to appoint Queen's Counsel, but that a Lieutenant-Governor appointed since the Union came into effect (1867) has no such power of appointment."*

In 1875 the Secretary of State for the colonies wrote :

"The Lieutenant-Governors of the Provinces of the Dominion, however important locally their functions may be, are a part of the Colonial administration staff, and are more immediately responsible to the Governor-General in Council. They do not hold commissions from the Crown ; and neither in power nor privilege resemble these Governors of Colonies, to whom after special con sideration of their fitness, the Queen under the great seal and her own hand and signet delegates portions of her prerogatives, and issues Her own instructions."

Sir John A. Macdonald, in his report as to Marriage Licenses in 1869, speaking of Lieutenant-Governors, says :

"They do not hold their appointment directly from the Queen, but are appointed by the Governor-General in Council pursuant to the 58th Section of the Act. Their powers are simply those conferred on them by Statute, and they have no right to deal with matters of prerogative as representative of the Sovereign."

The Hon. Mr. Fournier, Minister of Justice, was of opinion that neither the Lieutenant-Governor nor a Provincial Legislature has any power under the Statute to deal with the prerogatives of the Crown : and not being empowered to assent in the Queen's name to any law of a Provincial Legislature, he cannot bind Her

---

* The English Law officers of the Crown were of opinion in this case that the Legislature of a Province can confer by Statute on its Lieutenant-Governor the power of appointing Queen's Counsel. In Lenoir *vs.* Ritchie in the Supreme Court (not yet reported) there are *dicta* to the contrary.

Majesty's prerogative right. The members of
the Supreme Court appear to be of this opinion.*

As to the Lieutenant-Governors of the Provinces, except Ontario and Quebec, the Act
defines nothing as to their powers, authorities
and functions beyond the recommendation as
to money votes, and provisions as to assent,
disallowance and reservation of Bills, which are
the same as the provisions for the other Lieutenant-Governors.

---

* In the report of Mr. Justice Gwynne's Judgment in Lenoir *vs.* Ritchie
just come to hand, the learned Judge uses this language in reference to
the position of a Lieutenant-Governor: "The head of their Executive
Government is not an officer appointed by her Majesty, or holding any
commission from her, or in any manner personally representing her, but
an officer of the Dominion Government appointed by the Governor-General acting under the advice of a Council, which the Act constitutes the
Privy Council of the Dominion."

CHAPTER XXVI.

The Legislature in each Province is composed of a Lieutenant-Governor and Legislative Assembly, and in some of the Provinces a Legislative Council as well as an Assembly.

The powers of the Legislature are confined to a certain prescribed set of subjects, and need not be adverted to again.* The procedure in legislating is almost as intricate and elaborate as in the Parliament at Ottawa, from which it is necessarily copied. In those Provinces which have no Legislative Council, the Bills have of course to pass through their usual stages in one House only. The provisions relating to the election of a Speaker originally, and on vacancies, the duties of the Speaker, the absence of the Speaker, the quorum, and the mode of voting, are the same in the Ontario and Quebec Legislatures as in the Canadian House of Commons. The Legislatures of New Brunswick and Nova Scotia were, subject to the Provisions of the Act, left as they were before 1867. The same applies to Prince Edward Island and British Columbia, both of which had Legislatures before their admission into the

_____

* See chapter on the Powers of Parliament.

9

Union.   All the Provinces have power over their own Constitution, except as regards the office of the Lieutenant-Governor.

The provisions in the Act relating to Appropriations and Tax Bills, the recommendation of money votes, the assent, allowance and reservation of Bills, apply to all the Provinces substituting the Lieutenant-Governor for Governor-General, and the Governor-General for the Queen. The Lieutenant-Governors, on a Bill being presented to them, shall, according to their discretion, but subject to the provisions of the Act, declare that they assent thereto in the Governor-General's name, or that they withhold the Governor-General's assent, or that they reserve the Bill for the signification of the Governor-General's pleasure.*

A Bill reserved by the Lieutenant-Governor for the signification of the pleasure of the Governor-General in Council shall not have any force unless and until within one year from the day on which it was presented to the Lieutenant-Governor for the assent of the Governor-General, the Lieutenant-Governor signifies by speech or message to the House or Houses of his Legislature, or by proclamation, that it has received the assent of the Governor-General in Council.   Bills assented to by the Lieutenant-Governor may be

---

* Does the construction of the 55th Sec. of the Act, as interpreted by the 90th, contemplate instructions from the Governor-General to the Lieutenant-Governors on these points?

annulled by the Governor-General in Council within one year after an authentic copy of the Act has been sent to him.

The Governor in Council in the Dominion Parliament is said on very high authority to have the same controlling power over the Provincial Legislatures that the Imperial Parliament has over the Dominion. The extent of Provincial subordination. however, is not to be misunderstood. Both the Provinces and the Dominion have their own defined, ascertained limits ; and so long as they keep within these they can constitutionally enact what laws they please without reference to each other.

The two jurisdictions cover the same territory, but they embrace different objects. There are two checks on the Provinces—the Courts and the disallowing power of the Governor-General in Council. The power of disallowing Provincial Acts rests with the Central and not with the Imperial Government, as in the case of disallowing Dominion Acts ; but this will always be considered a harsh exercise of power unless in cases of great and manifest necessity, or where the Act is so clearly beyond the powers of the Local Legislature that the propriety of interfering would at once be recognized. It will always be very difficult for the Federal Government to substitute its opinion instead of that of the Legislative Assemblies in regard to matters within their

* Per C. J. Richards, in Severn vs. the Queen, 2 S. C. Reports, 96.

Provinces without exposing itself to be reproached with threatening the independence of the Provinces.*

The powers of the Courts are ones to be exercised with the most deliberate caution. Unless it is clear that the Legislature has transcended its authority, the Courts will not interfere. No Court can pronounce any Act of its Legislature void for any supposed inequality or injustice in its operation, provided it be on a subject matter purely within the scope of Legislative authority, and the provisions of the law in general.† It is the duty of the Judiciary, as the appropriate means of securing to the people safety from Legislative aggression, to annul all Legislative action without the pale of our written Constitution. In matters of conflict between the powers of the Local and Central Legislatures, the position of the Judiciary is not that of a subordinate, but of a co-ordinate branch of the Government; and it must declare every Act of the Legislature which is repugnant to the Constitution to be absolutely void. This power is not confined to any particular Court, but extends to all, both Dominion and Provincial. The language of Mr. Justice Story, as applied to his own country, no doubt applies equally here :

"The right of all Courts, State and National, to declare Unconstitutional laws void, seems settled beyond the reach of Judicial Controversy."

---

* Mr. Justice Fournier, in Severn vs. the Queen, 2 S. C. Reports.

† Sedgwick on Constitutional Law, and see McCullough vs. the State of Maryland—4 Wheaton.

They are the custodians of the Constitutions, the final depositories of power in this regard. They are to execute what is the law of the land, and it is no concern of theirs by or under what authority it has been enacted. The Union of the Provinces in 1867 did not in itself effect any alteration in these Courts in this respect.

It may be remarked here that these Courts are also bound to execute all laws in force in the Dominion, whether they are enacted by the Parliament of the Dominion or by the Local Legislatures.* The Provincial Courts are no mere Local Courts for the administration of the Laws passed by the Local Legislatures of the Provinces in which they are organized.

---

* See the Montmorency Election Case, S. C., not yet reported.

The Lieutenant-Governor and the Legislative Assembly of Ontario form the Legislature of that Province.

The Lieutenant-Governor is appointed by the Governor-General in Council, and holds office for five years, unless sooner removed for cause assigned. He is the Chief Officer of the Executive in the Provinces and the Head of the Legislature. The Provincial Legislatures have no power over him or his office, although in theory he may be supposed to act only upon their advice. He is a corporation sole, and may appoint a Deputy for certain purposes, such as executing Marriage Licenses, money warrants, and commissions under any Provincial Statute. He nominates as Executive Council of the Province such persons as he thinks fit, in number not to exceed six. In his absence, illness, or other inability, the Governor-General may appoint an Administrator to execute his office and functions. He summons and calls together the Legislature in the Queen's name, and may dissolve the same within the four years of its duration.

The Assembly is now composed of eighty-eight members; and for the purposes of representation the Province is divided up into this number of Electoral Districts or Ridings. These do not correspond to the Electoral Districts in Ontario which send members of Parliament to the House of Commons at Ottawa ; and, again, neither of these divisions corresponds with the Division of the Province into Counties for Municipal or Judicial purposes. Every County is a County for Municipal purposes (to be noticed hereafter), and sends at least one member to the Local and Federal houses ; but sometimes two or more Counties are united for Judicial purposes.

Members of the Local Legislature require no real property qualification, and are elected for four years. No Senator, Privy Councillor of the Dominion who is a member of the Commons, or any member of the Commons, can hold a seat in this House ; no person accepting or holding any office, commission or employment under the Crown by Provincial or Dominion appointment, and to which office any salary or fee, allowance, or emolument in lieu of salary, is attached, can be a member—except those members of the Executive office who are the leaders of the Government of the Province ; and with these exceptions, no person accepting or holding such office, commission or employment of profit as well under Provincial or Dominion appointment, or under any head of a Department in the Provincial Government, is eligible, no matter whether such profit be payable or not out of the public funds.

But any Army, Navy, or Militia Officers

(except Militia Staff Officers receiving permanent salaries), and any Justice of the Peace, and any Notary Public, may, unless otherwise disqualified, be members of the Legislative Assembly. No public contractor is eligible to sit or vote in the House ; and any disqualified person who does so shall forfeit the sum of $2,000 per day for so doing.

The Executive Council of Ontario is composed now of six members, who are appointed under the Great Seal of the Province, and hold office during pleasure. These members are selected from the following offices, some one member always taking two departments :—

1. Attorney-General for the Province.
2. A Secretary and Registrar of the Province.
3. A Treasurer of the Province.
4. A Commissioner of Crown Lands.
5. { A   "   Agriculture.
   { A   "   Public Works.
6. A Minister of Education.

Any of the powers and duties assigned by law to any of the officers constituting the Executive Council may, by order of the Lieutenant-Governor in Council, be transferred to any of the other officers, by name or otherwise. No member of this Council can sit or vote as a member of the Commons of Canada without forfeiting his office as Councillor.

The Executive Councillors are the Administration or Ministry of the Province—the Provincial Privy Council so to speak—and they form the

Government of the day. Besides being the choice of the Lieutenant-Governor they must have the support of a majority in the Legislative Assembly. They hold office during pleasure of both the Lieutenant-Governor and the Assembly; but it may be said that the choice of the Assembly will always hereafter guide the Lieutenant-Governor's choice. He has the undoubted right to dissolve the House and to dismiss Ministers having a majority at their back; but he does that always at great risk to himself. and probably with serious results to his Province. The procedure and line of conduct of the Local Legislatures has been copied so diligently from the Parliaments of Canada and Great Britain, that in case a Lieutenant-Governor follows the analogous power of the Crown in these places, he will content himself to follow the advice of his responsible Ministers rather than attempt to find Ministers supporting his own opinions. They are the choice of the Provincial members and answerable to the people—he is neither answerable to the Province nor its choice. If it be a question who is to rule on any occasion, the people affected have no right to complain if the determination is left in the hands of their own appointees.

Assuming, therefore, that Provincial Government is carried on by its Executive Council advising the Chief Executive Officer, a great portion of what has been said as to change of

Ministry, Cabinet, &c., in the foregoing chapters applies to the Provincial Constitutions.

The Departments in Ontario are six, and the duties of their Heads will be noticed presently. The procedure as to Bills, Orders, &c., is as nearly similar to the House of Commons as can be. A Bill here has to pass through the same stages, though only through one Assembly, there being no Upper House or Legislative Council in this Province. The Lieutenant-Governor then may assent to a Bill, or dissent from it, or reserve it for the consideration of the Governor-General, as has been already explained. He recommends all money votes, opens, prorogues, and dissolves the House, issues orders in Council, Proclamations, &c.

The House meets every year at Toronto, and is presided over by a Speaker appointed by the members. Not more than twelve months must intervene between the last sitting in one session and the first sitting in the next session.

Twenty members in the House are the smallest number capable of transacting business or forming a quorum. The Speaker may be one of this number. The conduct of business, the rules of debate, the regulation and management of the House, questions of proceedings, &c., are regulated by the House ; and in all unprovided cases the rules, usages and forms of the House of Commons in England are followed. The provisions relating to the first election of Speaker, the absence of the Speaker, quorum, and mode of voting, are the same in the Provincial Legislature of Ontario as in the House of Commons for Canada.

The House is not organized till the Speaker is chosen ; and there is no vacancy in the office till such choice has been made and the office has been filled, and that in the first meeting of the Assembly after a general election. Before the election of Speaker the Clerk of the House is substituted for the Speaker ; and the Clerk has no casting vote in case of an equality of votes for Speaker. No one can vote in the election of Speaker but a member of the Assembly, which the Clerk is not. In case the House was equally divided in the election of a Speaker, no one would be appointed.*

All laws in force in the late Province of Canada, all Courts of Civil and Criminal Jurisdiction. and all legal commissions, powers and authorities, and all officers, Judicial, Administrative and Ministerial, continue in Ontario and the other Provinces, as if the Union had not been made, subject, as to Imperial Legislation, to be repealed, abolished or altered by the Parliament of Canada, or the Legislature of the Provinces, according as they possess the power.

---

* Opinion of Hon. J. H. Cameron.

CHAPTER XXVIII.

ATTORNEY-GENERAL'S DEPARTMENT.

THERE are no statutory regulations as to the duties of the Attorney-General of Ontario, or the work performed in his office or department.

He is the Legal adviser of the Crown, and of the Executive Council or Ministry; and all legislation for the Province is conducted in his name and under his responsibility.

He appears on behalf of the Crown in civil and criminal cases; and he is the proper officer to enforce criminal laws by prosecution in the Queen's name in Courts of Justice in the Province. The Attorney-General of this Province is the officer of the Crown who must be considered to be present in the Courts of the Province to assert the rights of the Crown and those who are under its protection.*

His duties are somewhat analogous to those of the Minister of Justice at Ottawa; and he has all the rights, powers, duties, functions, responsibilities and authorities which, up to 1867, were vested in or imposed on the Attorney-General or Solicitor General of the Province of Canada by virtue of any Law, Statute, or Ordinance of Up-

---

Mr. Justice Strong (as Vice Chancellor) in Attorney-General vs. The Niagara Falls Bridge Company, 20 Chy., 34.

per Canada or Canada, and not repugnant to the Confederation Act of that year. This also applies to the other Executive officers in regard to their respective departments as mentioned hereafter, both in Ontario and Quebec.

2. PROVINCIAL SECRETARY AND REGISTRAR'S DEPARTMENT

This Department is under the control of the Provincial Secretary, but no express Statute has constituted it a department.

Reports on the Asylums, Prisons and Public Charities of the Province are returned from this Department every year; also reports relating to Tavern and Shop Licenses.

The bonds and securities required to be given by Public Officers are registered in the Registrar's Department, and returns made also in regard to them. The other matters upon which returns are made are the following :

The state of the Fee Fund, the expenses of the Administration of Justice, the number of Marriages, Births and Deaths, copies of all returns from the Clerks of the various Municipalities as to the population, real property, assessments, income and expenditure, liabilities, assets and property of their respective Corporations. A statement of the indebtedness of each Municipal Corporation at the close of the past year is made to the Lieutenant-Governor through the Provincial Secretary ; and a return also made to him from the sworn returns of the Clerks of each

Municipality of the number of resident ratepayers of the different Counties and Cities, and such Towns as are separated from Counties.

3. The Provincial Treasurer's Department.

All public moneys, from whatever source of revenue derived, and all moneys forming part of special funds administered by the Provincial Government, are paid in to the credit of the Provincial Treasurer. These revenues form what is called the Consolidated Revenue Fund of Ontario; and it is on the strength of the supplies of this Fund that the Lieutenant-Governor in Council can invest in Dominion Securities or Debentures whenever any surplus is not required for the public use of the Province.

The Treasurer of the Province lays every year before the House a Financial statement as to the assets and liabilities of the Province. He reports to the Lieutenant-Governor from the sworn returns of the Clerk of each Municipality (except County Clerks) as to the number of resident ratepayers and their indebtedness to the Municipal Loan Fund. He also reports as to the taxable property, and the resources and liabilities of each Municipal Corporation.

The Executive Government has charge of all fees and charges under the Act relating to Law Stamps; and the Provincial Treasurer procures the necessary stamps under the Act, keeps an account of all stamps, sells the same, and allows or may allow a commission of five per cent to those taking more than five dollars' worth.

The Treasurer has also certain statutory duties in reference to the Land tax in Algoma.

The moneys arising from the Clergy Reserves form a Separate Fund called "The Ontario Municipalities Fund;" and are paid into the Provincial Treasurer's Office, and paid out by him under orders in Council, or under the Act respecting Clergy Reserves. to the different Municipalities in Ontario, in proportion to their resident rate-payers, pursuant to the returns already referred to.

4. The Department of Crown Lands.

The Commissioner of Crown Lands presides over this Department; and he has the management and sale of the Public Lands and Forests belonging to the Province.

An Assistant Commissioner, appointed by the Lieutenant-Governor in Council, has charge of the Department in the absence of the Commissioner, or when a vacancy occurs in that office; and he performs such duties in the Department as may be assigned to him by the Lieutenant-Governor in Council, or the Commissioner of Crown Lands. Other officers may also be appointed in the same manner as the Assistant Commissioner.

The Department and office of the Surveyor-General are now transferred to this Department;

and the Commissioner exercises and performs such powers and duties as were assigned to or vested in that officer before the 17th of March, 1845.

The Commissioner of Crown Lands reports to the Legislative Assembly, within ten days after the meeting of the House, the proceedings, transactions and affairs of his office, during the preceding year.

The lands under the control of this Department are the Crown Lands, School Lands, Clergy Lands, and Mineral Lands. The Lieutenant-Governor in Council fixes the price, the terms and conditions of sale, and of settlement and payment of the Public Lands;* and the sales and appropriations of water lots, Licenses of occupation, and all assignments and the issue and cancellation of patents, are issued, registered and effected by the Commissioner, with other departmental business. He, or his Assistant, may issue Commissions, and may authorize those in the employ of the Department to take affidavits in reference to the business of the Department, or regarding which it is interested. He causes lists of patented lands to be forwarded to the different Registrars in the Province in the month of February in each year ; and also a list of land leased or licensed, or located as Free Grant. He advertises, if he thinks fit, lists of Public Lands for sale, and furnishes such other information as may be desirable.

---

* The Public Lands do not include Mineral Lands.

As to the Free Grant Lands, the Lieutenant-Governor in Council almost exclusively deals with these. The Act relating to Free Grants and Homesteads does not interfere with the power of the Commissioner to grant number of licenses in these lands; and any remission made by the Crown to settlers in occupation before 1872 in Free Grant lands may be made through the Commissioner in case it is so directed by Order in Council. The free grant territory lies within the districts of Algoma and Nipissing, and certain lands lying between the Ottawa river and the Georgian Bay.

The department looks after all trespasses to Public Lands, and has very full statutory instructions in regard thereto. It deals with the Mining lands of the Province, subject to such Orders in Council as may be made in reference to them and under the provisions of the General Mining Act.

When a claim is made as heir, devisee, or assignee of the nominee of the Crown, to the right to a Patent, Special Commissioners are appointed to decide thereon. These form what is called the Heir and Devisee Commission, which is one of the Courts of Law in Ontario.

If the patent has issued in error, or that the Commissioner has been misled, or for other good cause, the Court of Chancery has power to decree such Patent to be declared void.

5. THE DEPARTMENT OF AGRICULTURE.

This Department is in charge of the Commissioner of Agriculture and Arts, and the office is for the present combined with the Commissioner of Public Works.

The Bureau of Agriculture and Arts is attached to this Department; and the Lieutenant-Governor in Council appoints a Secretary, known as the Secretary of the Bureau of Agriculture and Arts, who conducts the Correspondence of the Department and such other business as may be assigned him by the Commissioner.

The Commissioner substitutes enquiries and collects useful facts and statistics relating to the Agricultural, Mechanical and Manufacturing interests of the Province, and adopts measures for disseminating or publishing the same in such manner and form as he finds best adapted to promote improvement within the Province, and to encourage immigration from other countries. He may appoint persons to inspect the books and accounts of any Society receiving Government Aid, and may examine witnesses and have documents produced in reference thereto.

The Societies in connection with the Department are : The Agricultural and Arts Association, all Agricultural and Horticultural Societies, and Mechanics' Institutes, the Association of Mechanics' Institutes of Ontario, the Fruit Growers Association of Ontario, the Entomolo-

gical Society of Ontario, the Dairymen's Association of Ontario, and the Ontario Society of
Artists. These make returns to this Department
and supply information on questions submitted
to them.

The Model Farm at Guelph, and a Library
and Museum in connection with it, are under the
control of the Commissioner ; and a Veterinary
College is established under prescribed rules of
the Council of the Agricultural and Arts Association, which also holds an Annual Provincial
Fair or Exhibition.

The Commissioner reports to the House of
Assembly, within 30 days after the opening of the
Session, a detailed and succinct report of the
proceedings in his Department.

6. The Department of Public Works.

This Department is presided over by the
Commissioner of Public Works, appointed by
Commission under the Great Seal.

The other officers, who are appointed by the
Lieutenant-Governor, are an Architect, an
Engineer, a Secretary, a Law Clerk, an Accountant, and such others, whether their
appointment be temporary or otherwise, as may
be necessary. The duties of the Architect,
Engineer, Secretary, Law Clerk, and Accountant,
are laid down by Statute.

The Commissioner has management of the
Department; and it is his duty to oversee and

direct the other officers and servants; and he
may have other duties also assigned him by
the Lieutenant-Governor in Council.

The Department has control of all land,
streams, water-courses, and property, real and
personal, heretofore or hereafter acquired for
the use of public works; all canals, locks, dams,
hydraulic works, harbour piers, and other works
for improving the navigation of any water;
all slides, dams, piers, booms, and other works
for facilitating the transmission of timber; all
hydraulic powers created by the construction of
any public works; all roads and bridges: all
public buildings; all railways and rolling stock
thereon: all vessels, dredges, scows, tools,
implements and machinery for the improvement of navigation; all drains and drainage
works; and all property heretofore or hereafter
acquired, constructed, repaired, maintained, or
improved, at the expense of the Province, and
not under the control of the Dominion Government. These are declared to be vested in Her
Majesty, and under the control of this Department.

Any other property, and any of these works,
roads, &c., purchased or constructed at the public expense, may, by Proclamation of the Lieutenant Governor, be vested in Her Majesty, and
subject to this Department.

Any property not required for the use of the
Public Works, may be leased or sold, under the

authority of the Lieutenant-Governor ; and for the purposes of the Department the Commissioner may acquire and take possession of any land or real estate, streams, waters, water courses, fences and walls, for specified purposes and under certain restrictions.

He has also the necessary powers as to drainage of land, and the construction of slides in mill-dams or embankments ; and he acts under the "Ontario Drainage Act" in reference to drains within Municipalities, on the request of their Councils, as provided by that Act. In case any township desire to undertake such work, the Commissioner, after the plans and estimates are submitted to the Department, can report thereon as to the investment of a portion of the Public money in debentures for the construction of such drainage for the benefit of such township.

All expenses connected with the provisions for preventing riots near Public Works are paid through the Commissioner under the statute respecting riots near Public Works. The sale of liquors near Public Works is prohibited by stringent provisions.

The Commissioner of Public Works must, within twenty-one days after the commencement of each session, make and submit to the Lieutenant-Governor an annual report on all the works under his control, shewing the state of each work, and the receipts and expenditure thereon, with such further information as may enable the Assembly to judge of the working of the Depart‑ ment.

7. Department of Education.

This Department consists of the Executive Council of the Province, or a Committee out of that number. One of the Executive Council is nominated to the office of Minister of Education by the Lieutenant-Governor.

The Minister of Education may hold any other office in the Executive Council, and he may be a member of the Legislative Assembly and sit and vote therein.

This Department supersedes the Council of Public Instruction, which was suspended on the 10th of February, 1876; and all the duties of that Council are transferred to this Department, with a Minister instead of the Chief Superintendent of Education at its Head.

The Education Department has certain duties and powers assigned to it. By it is prepared and presented the text books, studies and regulations as to High Schools, the regulation, organization, government and discipline of Public Schools, and the classification of schools and teachers. The efficiency of the Normal and Model Schools, the examination and certificates of teachers, the qualifications of inspectors and examiners, and the approval of text, prize and library books, are some of the many duties of the

Executive Council, or the Committee appointed
out of it as forming the Education Department.

The Minister has a number of Statutory duties
in connection with apportioning the Legislative
grants or funds to the different Public and High
Schools, and in reference to the general superintendence of the Normal Schools, the conduct
of Teachers, Institutes and regulations in respect
of text, library, prize books and other appliances
in School. He has large powers in the management of the Department under the Acts relating
to Public and High Schools.

Schools coming within the range of the
Separate Schools Act are subject to be inspected
by the Minister of Eductaion, and also to such
regulations as may be imposed on them from
time to time by the Education Department.

The Minister may also certify regarding any
proposed Industrial School in cities, that it is a
fit and proper one for the reception of children
to be sent there ; and the School shall thereupon
be deemed a certified Industrial School.

The Police Magistrate may send there such
children as apparently are under 14 years of
age if they are found begging, or receiving
alms, or are found wandering without any
visible means of support, and having no home,
or guardian, or any lawful business, or being
destitute, either as an orphan, or one whose
parent is imprisoned, or whose parents are so
vicious that they are under no proper control

or education ; or if such children are so un-
manageable that the parent or guardians
cannot control them. The rules of such School
are to be approved of by the Minister.

In cases in the Division Court, in which School
Inspectors, Trustees. Teachers or other persons
under these Acts are parties, an appeal is allowed
to the Superior Courts of law in Ontario. This
exceptional proceeding is for the purpose of
securing uniformity of decision in school matters.
The Minister has power also to submit a case to
any Judge of these Courts for the opinion or
decision of the Court therein.

The Minister of Education reports every year
to the Lieutenant-Governor in Council, up to the
31st of December, the actual state of the
Normal, Model, High and Public Schools, and
Collegiate Institutes, showing the Expenditure
and sources of revenue, with such statements
and suggestions, in reference to the improvement of the schools and the school law, and
promoting education, as he may deem useful
and expedient.

THE Legislature of Quebec consists of a Lieutenant-Governor and two Houses styled the Legislative Council of Quebec and the Legislative Assembly of Quebec.

The Legislative Council is composed of 24 members, who were appointed by the first Lieutenant-Governor of the Province in the Queen's name by Instrument under the Great Seal of Quebec. These hold office during life, unless the Legislature otherwise provides, subject to the Act of 1867. Their qualifications are the same as the Quebec Senators. These are different from the qualifications of other Senators in one respect only—that is in this way: Quebec was divided into 24 electoral divisions before Confederation; and each of these sent a Senator to Ottawa, and a Legislative Councillor to Quebec. Each must have his real property qualification in that division, or must be resident therein. The regulations as to vacancies in the place of a Legislative Councillor are the same as apply to Senators; and vacant seats are filled by the Lieutenant Governor in the same way as the first Councillors were appointed. Questions as to qualifications and vacancies in the Legislative Council are heard and determined by that body. The Lieutenant-Governor appoints their Speaker, and may remove him and appoint another. Ten members, including the Speaker, are a sufficient number to constitute a meeting for the exercise of its powers. The Speaker has a vote; and when the votes are equal, the motion is declared in the negative.

Every Legislative Councillor, before taking his seat, must take and subscribe before the Governor-General, or some one authorized by him, the Oath of Allegiance, and the Declaration of Qualification, prescribed for Senators as well, and referred to under the chapter in the Senate.

The Legislative Assembly of Quebec is composed of 65 members, until altered by the Legislature of the Province; and even then the second and third readings of a Bill for altering the limits of certain electoral divisions cannot be presented to the Lieutenant-Governor for his assent unless with the concurrence of the majority of the members representing all these divisions, and an address presented by the Assembly stating that the Bill has been so passed. Those Electoral Districts of Quebec, specially fixed, are the counties of Pontiac, Ottawa, Argenteuil, Huntington, Missisquoi, Beauce, Shefford, Stanstead, Compton, Wolfe and Richmond, Megantic, and the town of Sherbrooke.

The seat of Government is at Quebec; and the Executive Council is composed of the same officers, and in the same way as in Ontario, except that in Quebec the Speaker of the Legislative Council, and the Solicitor-General are included in the Executive. In Ontario there are no offices for such persons.

All the other provisions in the Act of 1867 relating to the Constitution, Legislative powers, and other matters specified therein, of Quebec are the same as have been set out in regard to Ontario.

The Judges of the Quebec Courts must be selected from the bar of that Province ; but when the laws relating to property and civil rights in Ontario, Nova Scotia and New Brunswick, are made uniform, the Governor-General may appoint Judges for these Provinces from any part of them.

The powers, authorities and functions of the Lieutenant-Governors are the same in both Provinces, except possibly in so far as the Legislatures of Upper and Lower Canada, prior to 1840, may have vested their respective Governors or Lieutenant-Governors with different powers, authorities and functions. The Legislature of Lower Canada was suspended at one time by Imperial Act, which did not happen to Upper Canada ; and this may have caused some slight difference in their statutory powers.

The Lieutenant-Governor of Quebec may, by Proclamation, constitute Townships in those parts of his Province not already constituted, and fix the metes and bounds thereof.

The Executive Government, as was seen, is carried on by the same number of members as in Ontario, except that they have no Minister of Education; but they have additional officers in the persons of the Solicitor General and Speaker of the Legislative Council.

The officers in charge of the Departments in Quebec succeed to all powers, duties and functions, &c., of those officers in the Government of the late Province of Canada, or of Lower Canada, in the same way as the Departmental Officers in Ontario do. The different offices in the Provinces agree in their main points, and are different chiefly in matters of detail; and it is not considered advisable in the present work to enter into a separate consideration of them.

CHAPTER XXX.

THE Act of 1867 uniting the Provinces did not alter the Legislatures of either Nova Scotia or New Brunswick. Subject to the Provisions of this Act they continued as they were before that date, and remain so until altered under the authority of the Act. The same applies to the Executive power of these Provinces, which was also unchanged. All the alterations they underwent were, in legislating only on the prescribed class of subjects assigned to the Provinces by such machinery as they always possessed. The mode of appointing the Governors was changed—it thereafter rested with the Governor-General of Canada. Nothing is said as to the powers, authorities and functions of any Lieutenant Governor, except those of Ontario and Quebec. All of them recommend to their respective Houses, by message, Appropriations and Tax Bills and all money votes. They can assent to Bills, disallow them, or reserve them for the signification of the Governor-General's pleasure.

These Provinces have the exceptional privilege of appointing Judges to their own Courts of Probate.

Nova Scotia and New Brunswick, like Quebec, have two Houses—a Legislative Council and a

Legislative Assembly. The Legislative Council in each Province is composed of 17 members. The House of Assembly in Nova Scotia is composed of 37 members, and in New Brunswick of 41 members.

The Executive Council in Nova Scotia is at present composed of nine members, of which only three have Portfolios—that is, the Provincial Secretary, the Attorney-General and the Commissioner of Mines and Works.

In New Brunswick the number of the Executive Council is nine also ; but here they have an Attorney-General, a Provincial Secretary and Receiver-General—a Chief Commissioner of the Board of Works, a Surveyor-General, and President of the Council.

CHAPTER XXXI.

THREE Provinces have been admitted into the Dominion of Canada since 1867. Of these, in order of time, Manitoba was admitted in 1870, British Columbia in 1871, and Prince Edward Island in 1873.

The Constitution originally given to Manitoba provided for a Lieutenant-Governor and two Houses, as in Quebec; but in 1876 the Legislative Council was abolished by the Local Legislature.

The Legislative Assembly, which, with the Lieutenant-Governor, now forms the Legislature, is composed of twenty members, representing the districts into which the Province is divided.

The Executive Council is composed of such persons and under such designations as shall seem fit to the Lieutenant-Governor. These at present consist of four persons—a Treasurer, a Provincial Secretary, Minister of Public Works, and the Attorney-General.

This Province and the Territories hereafter mentioned were part of Rupert's Land and the North-West Territory before they were admitted into the Union in 1870. This was effected by Proclamation pursuant to Order in Council at Ottawa. The boundary of Manitoba was defined then, but has been altered since, in 1877, by the Parliament of Canada, with the consent of the Legislature of Manitoba.*   All the provisions of the British North America Act which apply to the whole of the Provinces are applicable to Manitoba as if it had been one of the Provinces originally united by that Act.   The Act admitting this Province defines the qualification of voters—the duration of the Assembly to be four years, with a yearly session, as in Ontario, and the Seat of Government to be at Fort Garry, or within a mile of that place.

The provisions regarding the Speaker originally, and on vacancies, the duties of Speaker, the absence of Speaker, and the mode of voting, are the same as in the House of Commons at Ottawa. Canada assumes and defrays a large portion of the expenses of the Province. Almost every year since its admission a number of Acts have been passed in the Parliament of Canada applying to Manitoba.

---

* 40 Vict. (D) chap. 6.

CHAPTER XXXII.

BRITISH COLUMBIA.

THIS Province was admitted into the Union on the 20th of July, 1871, by Royal Proclamation of the Queen in Council.

The Constitution of their Legislature is the same as that of Ontario, being composed of a Lieutenant-Governor and one House of Assembly. The Executive is at present composed of an Attorney-General and Chief Commissioner of Lands and Works, a Provincial Secretary, and Minister of Finance, and a Legislative Assembly of twenty-five members.

CHAPTER XXXIII.

THIS Province was admitted into the Union on the 1st of July, 1873.

The Legislature is composed of a Lieutenant-Governor, a Legislative Council of 13 members, and a Legislative Assembly of 33 members—both Houses being elected by the people.

The Executive Council is composed of the Attorney-General, the Provincial Secretary and Treasurer, and the Commissioner of Public Works, with some other members without departments.

The terms upon which this Colony was admitted are laid down at considerable length in the Order in Council in that behalf. Canada became liable for the debts of the Province, and the Province was entitled to incur a liability of four millions of dollars in view of her isolated and exceptional condition, and as something towards the share other Provinces received from Canada in reference to Railways and Canals. There being no revenue from Crown Lands in the Province, the Dominion Government agreed to supply her with about $40,000 per annum in order to purchase lands from large landed proprietors. Canada also pays a large yearly sum towards defraying the expenses of the Local

Government and Legislature, besides such charges as are incident or appertaining to the general Government and allowed to the other Provinces.

The Constitution of the Legislative and of the Executive Government remained unchanged; but all the provisions of the Act of 1867, except those parts which in terms or by reasonable intendment apply to only one Province, or to a part of the Dominion, take effect in Prince Edward Island.

CHAPTER XXXIV.

THE NORTH-WEST TERRITORIES.

THESE Territories are composed of what was formerly " Rupert's Land" and the North-Western Territory, except such portions as were carved thereout to form the Province of Manitoba. What is called the North-West Territory includes geographically the tract of country lying between Manitoba and British Columbia. The tract of country lying east of Manitoba and west of Ontario is called the District of Keewatin.

The Parliament of Canada enacted regulations as to the government and legislation of these Territories.* For the North-West Territory there is a Lieutenant-Governor appointed, as other Lieutenant-Governors are ; and he administers the Government under instructions given him by order in Council or by the Secretary of State for Canada. An Administrator may be appointed during the absence, illness or other inability of the Lieutenant-Governor. A Council not to exceed six persons is appointed by the Privy Council of Canada to aid in administering the Government of the North-West Territories ; and the seat of Government, at present Battleford, is fixed (and, if necessary, changed) by order in Council also.

---

* 38 Vic. cap. 49; 40 Vic. cap. 7.

The Legislative Governor alone, or in Council, may, as soon as the Territory is provided with a Legislative Assembly, make such ordinances for the government of his Territories as the Governor in Council may from time to time confer on him, provided these are within the limits of legislation under the Act of 1867. The Dominion Acts in reference to these Territories also lay down regulations as to the formation of electoral districts, number of members in the Assembly, mode of voting, etc. ; and a number of enactments as to property, civil rights, and the administration of justice.

CHAPTER XXXV.

THE district of Keewatin is a portion of the North-west Territories, and was created in 1876. Its western boundary was then defined as lying east of Manitoba and north of the United States, and occupying the tract of land between that Province and Canada in the east and the Hudson Bay Territory.*

The Governor in Council may detach any portion of this district to the North-West Territories when it appears of public advantage to do so.

None of the provisions in the Acts respecting the North-West Territory apply to this District, unless, after 1876, reference is made therein to it.

The Lieutenant-Governor of Manitoba is *ex officio* Lieutenant-Governor of this district; and he, with a Council of not less than five or more than ten, administers the affairs of the district. The Council is appointed by the Privy Council at Ottawa; and all the powers it possesses are derived from Orders in Council there.

Provisions somewhat similar, and in many instances the same as were set out in the last chapter as to the Government of the North-West Territories, apply to this District; and all laws in force in the Territories are to remain in force in the District until otherwise altered.†

---

* Sec. 39 Vic., chap. 21 (D), as to boundary.   † Sec. 39 Vic., chap. 21 (D)

CHAPTER XXXVI.

THE PEOPLE.

SUBJECTS, ALIENS, DENIZENS.

We have hitherto considered the rulers, or governing powers, of the people of the Dominion of Canada ; we will now devote a small space to the ruled or governed—the people—whether subjects or aliens.*

A subject is defined to be one who is under the protection of and owes allegiance to the Sovereign or ruling power in the State. By British subjects are meant such as are born within the dominions of the Crown of England, or under the allegiance of the Queen.

There are many persons residing within the dominions of the Crown who are not subjects of Her Majesty ; and on the other hand there are many residing in foreign countries who are British subjects. All residents who are not subjects, and all non-residents not British subjects, are aliens. Of the former class may be mentioned all those who belong to other countries, and who have not renounced their allegiance thereto, or rather who have not taken the oath of allegiance and became naturalized here. Foreign consuls and other representa-

* See the admirable collection of cases as to aliens in Mr. Hodgins' Manual of Voters' Lists.

tives of foreign nations, though resident here, are not British subjects. Nor are those such who are simply domiciled here as travellers or agents. In the same way our consuls and representatives abroad are yet British subjects, though non-residents; and so are all British-born subjects who, living abroad, have not renounced their British nationality. Children born out of the Dominions of the Crown, whose father and mother were at the time of their birth in allegiance with the Queen, are subjects; and the children of all natural-born subjects, no matter where born, are also subjects of Her Majesty. In other words, the second generation of children from British parents are subjects; but it is doubtful if this extends to the third generation. If the grand-father by the father's side was a British subject, the grand-children would be British subjects also, according to Blackstone. Out of ten of the most eminent lawyers in England, five were of opinion in a case since Blackstone's time against the right of one whose grand-father had been born out of the British dominions to inherit land in England; and the other five were of a contrary opinion. So far as land in Canada is concerned an Alien has the same capacity as a British subject to take by gift, conveyance, descent, devise or otherwise howsoever; and to hold, possess, enjoy, claim, receive, convey, devise, impart and transmit real estate therein the same as a natural-born or naturalized subject of Her Majesty.

The real estate of aliens in this country accordingly descends or is transmitted the same as if owned by a subject. Aliens in Ontario enjoy all the privileges in regard to Acts relating to Building Societies and Joint Stock Companies for supplying cities, towns and villages with gas and water. But an alien cannot serve as a juryman in any Court, nor is he entitled to be the owner of a British ship.

Every child born within the dominions of the Crown is a British subject for all purposes, and while resident therein cannot by any act of his divest himself of such character. But a British-born subject, if a subject of another State at the time of his birth (as may be the case with ambassadors' children), can cease to be a British subject by making certain declarations prescribed by the Imperial Statutes of 1870 and 1872 in reference to these matters. Any subject, if under no disability, may voluntarily become naturalized in a foreign State, and thus cease to be a British subject. This is expatriation.

An alien may become a British subject by Naturalization and in other ways,

Every alien-born woman becomes naturalized by marrying a British natural-born or naturalized subject.

Every other alien who comes to reside in the Dominion of Canada with intent to settle therein, and remains for three years, can, by taking the oaths of residence and allegiance, become a naturalized citizen.

The following are the oaths of Residence and Allegiance :

OATH OF RESIDENCE.

" I, A. B., do swear (*or, being one of the persons allowed by Law to affirm in judicial cases*, do affirm) that I have resided three years in this Dominion, with intent to settle therein, without having been during that time a stated resident in any foreign country. So help me God."

OATH OF ALLEGIANCE.

" I, A. B., do sincerely promise and swear (*or, being one of the persons allowed by Law to affirm in judicial cases*, do affirm) that I will be faithful and bear true allegiance to Her Majesty Queen Victoria, as lawful Sovereign of the United Kingdom of Great Britain and Ireland, and of the Dominion of Canada, dependent on and belonging to the said United Kingdom, and that I will defend her to the utmost of my power against all traitorous conspiracies and attempts whatever which shall be made against Her Person, Crown and Dignity ; and that I will do my utmost endeavour to disclose and make known to Her Majesty, Her Heirs and Successors, all treasons and traitorous conspiracies and attempts which I shall know to be against Her or any of them ; and all this I do swear without any equivocation, mental evasion, or secret reservation. So help me God."

The oaths can be administered by a Judge or Justice of the Peace ; and a certificate is granted and filed in Court, after which, if no objection is sustained as to its validity the alien becomes a British subject as much as if he or she was born in Canada, subject to some exceptions in the English Act relating to naturalization.* Every alien who had a settled place of abode in either of the Provinces of Ontario, Quebec, Nova Scotia, or New Brunswick, before the 1st of July, 1867, and who is still a resident of the same, is deemed to be a British subject for all purposes, provided in the case of males, they take the prescribed oath of residence. Any person who, being within the Dominion prior to the 1st of January, 1868, took the necessary oaths of allegiance and residence also became naturalized.

There seems to be no difference between the rights and privileges of a national-born subject and a naturalized subject. In England at one time the latter could not be a Privy Councillor or member of Parliament, or hold any of the great offices of State ; but he is now entitled to all political and other rights, powers and privileges, and is subject to all obligations to which a natural-born British subject is entitled or subject. In case a naturalized British subject returns to his own country, he loses the character of British subject unless he renounced his original nationality in pursuance of the laws of the State, or in pursuance of a Treaty to that effect.

The certificate of naturalization granted in the United Kingdom confers no rights or privileges upon an alien in Canada.†

---

* 33 Vic. chap. 14, Imp. Act.

† Earl Carnarvon's Circular Despatch to the Colonies, Sept., 1871.

Besides subjects and aliens there is a third class called Denizens, who, by means of letters patent from the Crown, enjoy certain rights of citizenship as long as they remain within the Dominion. It is a sort of middle state between subject and alien. In England a denizen cannot hold any high office of State, and can neither inherit or devise land, and only take by purchase. In Canada, whatever significance the term may have, a denizen must at least have equal powers and rights as to real estate with a subject; and he has, no doubt, the additional rights of voting and holding such offices as his patent allows him. The existence of such persons is contemplated at all events, as there is mention made of denizens in some of the Statutes.

The consideration as to whether any person is a subject or not becomes material in relation to certain offences against the Crown. None but a subject can be found guilty of treason; or rather what is treason in a subject may be no more than a felony in a foreigner. The general law as to what offences are to be adjudged treason, as laid down in the 25th year of King Edward III., is the law on the subject here; and is set out in an Act relating to the security of the Crown, 31 Vic., cap. 69 (1868) D.

The regulations as to titles and precedence in Canada are inserted here, and may be found useful for reference :

TITLES UNDER CONFEDERATION.

1. The Governor-General of Canada to be styled "His Excellency."

2. The Lieutenant Governors of the Provinces to be styled "His Honor."

3. The Privy Councillors of Canada to be styled "Honorable," and for life.

4. Senators of Canada to be "Honorable," but only during office, and the Title not to be continued afterwards.

5. Executive Councillors of the Provinces to be styled "Honorable," but only while in office, and the Title not to be continued afterwards.

6. Legislative Councillors in the Provinces not in future to have that Title ; but gentlemen who were Legislative Councillors at the time of the Union, to retain their Title of "Honorable" for life.

7. The President of the Legislative Council in the Provinces to be styled "Honorable" during office.

8. The Speakers of the House of Assembly in the Provinces to be styled "Honorable" during office.

TABLE OF PRECEDENCE WITHIN THE DOMINION OF CANADA.

1. The Governor-General, or officer administering the Government.

2. Senior Officer commanding Her Majesty's Troops within the Dominion, if of the rank of a General ; and officer commanding Her Majesty's Naval Forces on the British North American Station, if of the rank of an Admiral. Their own relative rank to be determined by the Queen's Regulations on this subject.

3. The Lieutenant-Governor of Ontario.

4.	"	"	Quebec.
5.	"	"	Nova Scotia.
6.	"	"	New Brunswick.

7. Archbishops and Bishops according to seniority.

8. Members of the Cabinet according to seniority.

9. The Speaker of the Senate.

10. The Chief Justice of the Supreme Court.

11. The Chief Judges of the Courts of Law and Equity, in accordance with the date of their respective Commissions.

12. Members of the Privy Council, not of the Cabinet.

13. General Officers of Her Majesty's Army serving in the Dominion, and officers of the rank of Admiral in the Royal Navy serving on the British North American Station, not being the Chief Command; the relative rank of such officers to be determined by the Queen's Regulations.

14. The Officer commanding Her Majesty's Troops in the Dominion, if of the rank of Colonel or inferior rank, and the Officer commanding Her Majesty's Naval Forces on the British North American Station, if of equivalent rank; their relative rank to be ascertained by the Queen's Regulations.

15. Members of the Senate.

16. Speaker of the House of Commons.

17. Puisne Judges of the Supreme Court in accordance with the dates of their respective commissions.

18. Puisne Judges of Courts of Law and Equity according to seniority.

19. Members of the House of Commons.

20. Members of the Executive Council (Provincial) within their Province.

21. Speaker of the Legislative Council within his Province.

22. Members of the Legislative Council within their Province.

23. Speaker of the Legislative Assembly within his Province.

24. Members of the Legislative Assembly within their Province.

Retired Judges of whatever Court take precedence next after the present Judges of their respective Courts.

The new regulations respecting the precedence of naval officers, the subject of salutes, or of the precedence to be given to Lieutenant-Governors within their Provinces or at the Seat of Government, have not yet been received.*

---

* See Letter of Sir Michael Hicks-Beach to His Excellency the Marquis of Lorne, Nov. 3, 1879.

CHAPTER XXXVII.

I. REPRESENTATION.

THE privilege of taking part in the Government of one's country by being represented in Parliament, or represented in the Legislatures or Municipalities which make our laws, is one of the most valued rights of a free people. The right of the citizens to have a voice in every matter that affects their liberties is called their Franchise. But to have a voice or vote in such matters is not accorded to every body. Certain qualifications are necessary, and these qualifications vary.

Where every citizen is entitled to vote it is called Universal Suffrage—voting being the right of suffrage.

The system of representation which prevails in Canada, from the highest delegate of the people in the Commons down through the Provincial and Municipal elections, is based on divisions of the population; though territory or certain areas of land are so connected with this that the latter are represented as well. While it is true that every acre of land is represented, the manner of its being so represented is arrived at with regard to the number of people. Numbers of people possessing no land qualification are represented by virtue of the income tax, or, as in Ontario, under the Farmers' Sons Act. While it it is strictly true that our system of representation regards both population and territory, the real basis is the population. The territory is an accident of the voters, and in itself is not entitled to representation. The third way, or representation by class representation, though much talked of in other countries, cannot be said to enter into the idea of the Canadian or English system.

THE COMMONS.

Of the 204 members in this House, each of the Provinces is represented by their respective members, and each Province is divided up into constituencies or ridings having regard to the population and areas therein. The *number* of divisions into which the Provinces are divided up for electing members to their legislatures is the same as for the Dominion elections in most Provinces; but the *areas* of these divisions are generally different. The qualifications of voters are the same in the Provincial and Dominion elections; so that any one entitled to vote for a member of his Provincial Legislature can vote for a member of the House of Commons in that Province.

It would be beside the scope of this little work to attempt any exact epitome of the qualifications necessary for voters in the different Provinces, and what offices and positions disqualify

persons from voting. Some remarks as to
Ontario may be desirable however.

In this Province the persons not permitted to
vote are : 1. All Judges of any of our Courts, and
all Clerks of the Peace, County Attorneys, Registrars, Sheriffs, Deputy Sheriffs, and Deputy
Clerks of the Crown. 2. All Agents for the sale
of Crown Lands. 3. All Officers of the Customs
of the Dominion, and all Officers employed in the
collection of any duties payable to Her Majesty
in the nature of duties of Excise ; and 4. All
Postmasters in Towns and Cities.   Any of these
persons voting shall forfeit $2,000, and his vote
is null and void. 5. No Returning Officer,
Election Clerk, or paid Election Agent, shall be
entitled to vote ; but this does not apply to the
Deputy Returning Officers or Poll Clerks, who
are paid under the provisions of the Act. 6.
Lastly, no woman can vote at any election.

Subject to these exceptions every person being
of the full age of 21 years and a subject of Her
Majesty by birth or naturalization, if duly entered
in the list of voters to be used at the pending
election, and if not otherwise by law prevented
from voting, is entitled to vote for members for
the Legislative Assembly of Ontario.

1. In order to entitle a person to be entered
on the voters' lists, he must be interested in
real property as owner, tenant, or occupant, to
the extent of $400 in Cities, $300 in Towns, and
$200 in incorporated Villages or Townships.   If

he ceases to have such interest he may still have a vote, provided his name is entered in the Revised Assessment Roll, and that he is a resident of the Electoral District.

In regard to the value of the property if vested in joint owners, if there is sufficient when divided to give each a vote, each has one ; if not, none of the owners has a vote. And so if three persons in a city are assessed for $1,200, each has a vote ; if assessed for $1,000, none of them can vote.

2. Persons residing continuously in the Local Municipality since the completion of its last Revised Assessment Roll, and who, being assessed on an *income* of $400 at least, and have paid their last year's taxes, are entitled to vote.

3. *Farmers' Sons* resident on their father's or mother's farm for twelve months prior to the return of the Assessment Roll, and who are rated for an amount sufficient to qualify them, can vote. Where there are a number of sons the provisions, as to one or more voting, are somewhat similar as to joint owners of real estate, except that the division of the property enures to qualifying as many of the parties in the order of their age as the value of the property or the number of the sons will permit of.

4. All *Indians*, or persons part Indian, if duly enfranchised and possessing the same qualifications as other persons in their electoral districts, are entitled to vote.

5. In Algoma, Parry Sound, and some other exceptional places, every male person being twenty-one years of age, a naturalized subject and not otherwise disqualified, and who, at the time of the election, is the owner of real estate where he tenders his vote, to the value of $200, or who is and has been for the preceding six months a resident householder, is entitled to vote.

[The reader is referred to a Manual of Voters' Lists by Mr. Hodgins, Q. C., for full information on this subject.]

2. Public Meetings.

PUBLIC opinion is frequently expressed through the medium of Public meetings, which, so long as they remain orderly, are privileged to discuss almost any subject. It is the undoubted right of subjects to meet together in a peaceable and orderly manner for the consideration and discussion of matters of public interest, or for making known their views to Her Majesty or Her Representative in the Dominion or in the Provinces, either in approbation or condemnation of Public matters.

Public meetings, in order to enable them to the recognition of the Law, must be called by certain persons and in a particular way.

In any city or town, on the requisition of any twelve citizens entitled to vote for members of the Local Legislature, a meeting may be called by the Sheriff or by the Mayor or other Chief Municipal officer, which is a Public meeting under the Act and entitled to the protection accorded to such meeting. The requisitionists must have a property qualification in the town or city in which the meeting is to be called, and their property must be within the particular district, ward, or parish, whose inhabitants call the meeting. Two resident Justices of the Peace appear also to have the power to call Public meetings. The notice or summons calling together a Public meeting must issue ten days before the meeting; must set forth the names of the requisitionists, or at least 12 of them; must state that the meeting is called in conformity with the provisions of the Act; and that the meeting and all persons attending the same are to take notice of that fact, and govern themselves accordingly.

Whoever calls such meeting, at least in Ontario, must remain; and whether presiding over it or not, help to preserve the peace thereat. Special constables may be appointed, and the military force, if necessary, brought to his assistance. Should a meeting of 12 or more become disorderly the Mayor, Sheriff, Magistrate, Justice of the Peace, or other officer, can read the Proclamation set out in what is commonly called the Riot Act; and if, after the lapse of an hour, they do not disperse, he can forcibly break up the meeting, using the Civil and Military assistance as has been mentioned. The original of our Act relating to Riots and Riotous Assemblies was passed in England in the reign of King George I. The Canadian Act is 31 Victoria, cap. 70 (1868), and the proclamation to be read before using any violent measures is as follows :

"Our Sovereign Lady the Queen chargeth and commandeth all persons being assembled immediately to disperse themselves, and peaceably to depart to their habitations or to their lawful business, upon the pains contained in the Act respecting Riots and Riotous Assemblies. God save the Queen."

Such persons not obeying the command to disperse are guilty of felony and liable to be imprisoned in the penitentiary for life, or for any term not less than two years. or liable to be otherwise imprisoned for any term less than two years.

Powers are given to Justices of the Peace, Sheriffs, Mayors and others, to apprehend the offenders who do not disperse within one hour after the Proclamation is read; and persons engaged in suppressing the riot are justified even if the death of the rioter ensue from his resistance. Any persons opposing with force and arms any peace officer or other engaged in suppressing a riot, or any persons preventing the making of the Proclamation, are guilty of felony and liable to the same punishment as the rioters themselves.

3. PETITIONS TO PARLIAMENT.

PETITIONING is another mode of expressing public opinion, and by it persons or classes may be heard in Parliament or elsewhere when they conceive that their views were not fully set out by their representatives. It is about the only way of being heard that is left to those who are not voters. If no channel were left to the people, except through their representatives, it may well happen that the minority would never be heard, except in the disorders of riot or revolution. A class may be interfered with, or the Legislation may be too slow or too far in advance of the interests of the people. In these and many other instances petitioning is resorted to.

Every person, whether an elector or not; can petition to Parliament or to the Local Legislature ; but the petition must be presented by a member of the House, who is responsible that it does not contain impertinent or improper matter.

Petitions must be fairly written or printed ; and in the Senate three of the petitioners' names must appear on the sheet containing the petition. Petitions from Corporations must be duly authenticated by their Corporate Seal. Petitions signed by persons representing public meetings are received as from the persons whose names are affixed to the petition.

A member presenting a petition in the Commons must endorse his name thereon, and confine his remarks to a statement of the parties from whom the petition comes, the number of signatures attached, and the material allegations it contains. Petitions are laid on the table by direction of the Speaker without debate in reference thereto : but if required, the Clerk may read them, and if they complain of any personal grievance requiring an immediate remedy the matter may be at once discussed. There does not appear to be any Canadian Legislation as to petitions to Parliament ; but the fact that those presenting them are responsible for their propriety, sufficiently insures their being consistent with the dignity of Parliament. It is probable that the English Act for the prevention of Tumultuous petitioning to Parliament is in force in Canada.

CHAPTER XL

LIBERTY OF THE PRESS.

THE Press is the greatest means of expressing public opinion. In Canada its liberty is not restrained by any State censorship. Beyond the occasional intervention of aggrieved parties taking advantage of the law of LIBEL, the press is allowed to correct itself, and proceeds somewhat on the principal that the legal doctrine of set-off may be made to work in the matter of abuse and recrimination as well as in more appropriate subjects.

Libel as a *crime* is governed by a uniform law in the Dominion, and is punishable by fine or imprisonment, or both.

Any person publishing, or threatening to publish, any libel upon any other, or directly or indirectly threatening to print or publish, or abstain from so doing, or offers to prevent the same with intent to extort any money or security for money, or any valuable thing, or with intent to induce any person to confer upon or procure for any person any appointment or office of profit or trust, is guilty of a misdemeanor, and liable to a fine not exceeding $600, or to imprisonment with hard labor for any period less than two years, or liable to both, as the Court may award.

Whoever maliciously publishes any defamatory libel, knowing it to be false, may be fined any sum less than $400, or imprisoned, as in the other cases, or both. Other defamatory libels are punished by imprisonment of one year or less, with a fine not exceeding $200. The truth of any libelous matter is no defence, unless it was for the public benefit that it should be published.

Libel as a *civil* action is not uniformly defined, but is left to be determined by the Provincial Legislatures. The punishment then is the amount of damage supposed to be suffered by the aggrieved party, which amount is found by a jury. In the criminal actions the jury simply finds whether or not the accused is guilty of the charge preferred against him : in the civil action the jury finds generally if there was a libel ; and if so, what damage was sustained by the plaintiff.

Besides matters which are brought into Public notice by means of the Press, of Public meetings, and of Petitions, the Governor in Council has the right to institute Commissions of Enquiry into Public matters concerning any matter connected with the good government of Canada, or the conduct of any part of the Public business. The Commissioners appointed in this way may have conferred on them the power of summoning before them any party or witness, and requiring them to give evidence on oath, or by affirmation, orally or in writing, and to produce all documents and things requisite for the full investigation of the matters into which they are appointed to examine. These Commissioners may also have the same power given them as are vested in any Court of Law in Civil cases to compel the attendance of witnesses.

Similar powers are given to the Lieutenant-Governor of Ontario, and in some other Provinces, as to Commissions of Enquiry.

LOCAL ADMINISTRATIVE GOVERNMENT.

On much the same principle as the Dominion is divided up into Provinces, with power to each of those to manage their own internal affairs, the Provinces have generally divided themselves into Municipal Corporations, with large powers of directing their own domestic concerns. While the Legislature presides over the Corporations, these latter have certain rights guaranteed to them, and in the exercise of which, within legitimate limits, they are free to manage their own local affairs.

The Division of the Canadas into Townships and Counties dates back a long period. Alterations were frequently made in Counties for electoral or judicial purposes; but as to Municipal Corporations embracing a certain area few changes appear to have been made in those counties definitely bounded in the first Crown Survey. New Townships are frequently added in unsettled districts, and occasionally alterations made. The same applies to Townships. In Ontario certain limits are prescribed for Villages desiring Incorporation, and the population must be at least 750 persons. In the same way Towns must have 2,000 and Cities 5,000 inhabitants. These do not become Incorporated by the fact of having so many inhabitants. A Charter of Incorporation is granted them by the Lieutenant-Governor creating them Cities, Towns or Villages, as the case may be. Until Incorporated they belong to the County or Township.

The local affairs of these different Corporations are managed by a Council, which is the Municipal Legislature and the limit of their enactments ; or By-laws are prescribed by the Acts of the Local Legislature relating to Municipal Corporations. These By-laws are very comprehensive, and in Ontario include the obtaining of such real and personal property for the use of the Corporation as it may require, the appointment of necessary officers aiding agricultural or other kindred societies or incorporated mechanics' institutes, aiding manufacturing establishments, road companies, and also charities and indigent persons, taking the census of their municipality. regulating the driving on roads and bridges, the egress from public buildings, and very extensive powers as to drainage. They can impose fines up to $50 for neglect of duty or breach of these By-laws, and may distrain and sell the goods of the offender, and if necessary inflict reasonable punishment by imprisonment not exceeding 21 days.

The power of each of the different Municipal Corporations of cities, counties, towns and townships are very minutely set out in the Acts relating to Municipal Institutions. The different Municipal Corporations are composed of Aldermen or Councillors or Reeves and their Deputies, with a presiding officer who is the Mayor, Warden or Reeve as the case may be. These bodies form the Local Administration of their Municipalities, are elected for one year at a time, and must have certain property qualifications. They have certain specified powers, a regular system of procedure, and an Executive in some cases. They are restrained by the Superior Courts when these By-laws are in excess of their powers, and these Courts compel them to exercise their powers in proper cases if they refuse to do so. The Provincial Legislatures grant them their powers, but commit the proper execution of them to the controlling care of the Courts.

CHAPTER XLII.

LAW AND THE COURTS.

THE people of the Dominion have abundant Legislative machinery. Three Legislatures contribute more or less to regulate our internal economy or external relations. The boundaries of Imperial, Dominion, and Provincial Legislation have been adverted to before. Regarding the specific subjects assigned to the Canadian Legislatures by the British North America Act, it would seem that the Imperial Legislature has renounced its right to interfere in these matters. There is Imperial as well as Colonial authority for this position. The line of demarcation separating our law-making powers would apparently then be well defined, and the law on each class of subjects may be confidently looked for in one direction only.

So far as to statutory law since 1867.

The Statute books before that in the various Provinces must next be considered. These form an important source, as well for the laws they initiate as for those they introduce. Again, what is known as the Common or the Unwritten law of England was largely imported into all parts of the Dominion, in virtue not only of British subjects bringing part of this law with them of necessity, but also by means of its express introduction by statute. The introduction of English law in these various ways brought with it the decisions of the Courts in Great Britain in reference to the same ; and these decisions or precedents are another source of laws. The introduction of the Criminal law of England to the old Province of Quebec in 1774 introduced all these sources of law at once. •

In the Province of Ontario a few references will show how extensively the laws of England have been adopted here. In 1792 all the amendments made in England to the Criminal law since 1774 were transferred to Upper Canada ; and in the same year the law as to property, civil rights, and trial by jury as it then stood, was declared to be the law for the Province. On the establishment of the Court of Chancery, the law of England, as it stood in 1837, regarding the English Court of Chancery was, unless otherwise provided, to be in force here ; and the rights, incidents and privileges of the Courts of Common Law in England in 1859 were transferred to our Superior Courts of law.

The Local Legislatures may delegate to Municipal or other Corporations the power of making laws. This is effected by the by laws of these bodies, which are as much the law of the land as any Legislative Acts ; and as another example, may be mentioned the powers of the Governors in Council to promulgate orders having the force of laws.

When it is considered that all the different sources of the laws, their application and their meaning, have to be considered and determined by the Courts, it becomes material to consider the position and jurisdiction of our Judicial tribunals. This is the more necessary in this country, as it is apprehended that their position is relatively more important than in England, so far as the construction of Constitutional law is concerned.

In Great Britain the Legislature is the chief power in the land. There being no written Constitution, no plain speaking and inflexible statute of paramount law, under which the Government of the country is carried on, the Constitutionality of its Acts cannot be questioned by the Courts in the same way as in those countries wherein there is a written Constitution. The Acts of the Legislature form the law, which its Courts must execute without questioning their validity or testing them with the Constitution. The British people speak in each Legislative Enactment ; and their last utterance is the guide for their Courts, who are always subordinate to the Legislature, and who exist solely by their permission.

These Imperial enactments extend at times to the Colonies ; and there Her Majesty's Courts are precisely in the same position, so far as these enactments are concerned. They have the same duties under them as the British Courts have— to see that they are carried out according to law.

An Imperial Statute in 1867 gave Canada a written and defined Constitution. Under this Constitution numerous bodies were endowed with large Legislative powers. All the laws were to be executed by the Courts, but executed so as not to conflict with the Imperial laws, which must, first of all, be executed. Our Courts, therefore, while bound to execute all laws in force, must be the judges as to what laws are in force. A Canadian law which is repugnant to any Imperial enactment must be declared void by the Courts—a higher than Canadian power has said that it is no law at all. Again, the Dominion Parliament may usurp Provincial rights, or a Province assume to deal with Dominion matters; the Courts still sitting under the Constitution, the Imperial enactment must refuse to obey their behests. The Courts in Canada are still the Queen's Courts and bound to execute such law as is in force, but equally bound to declare that the Acts of any of our Legislatures, when transcending their limits, are unconstitutional and void. The Courts, so long as they are permitted to exist, are not the creatures of the Legislature ;

they are of course subordinate to constitutional
legislation, but they are co-ordinate and in effect
superior to that which is not constitutional.

This being, it is apprehended, the position of
our Judiciary in Canada, the laws to be considered necessarily refer to three sources: the
Imperial, the Dominal and the Provincial. The
first must be obeyed at all events; the other two
must be equally obeyed, provided they are
constitutional; and if not, they must be declared
void.

CHAPTER XLIII

The different Provinces of the Dominion make their own regulations under Legislative authority as to who are and who are not officers of their Courts, and their powers, duties and obligations. Reference will here be made to the chief officers engaged in and about the Courts.

In Ontario the Treasurer and Benchers of *The Law Society of Upper Canada* form a Corporation ; and they and their successors in office regulate the government of the Society, the appointment of officers, the legal education of students, and the term of studentship, and the admission of applicants as Barristers at Law or as Attorneys and Solicitors into the Law Society. The Benchers have the appointment of reporters to the Superior Courts, and fix the amount of their salaries.

No one can practice at the Bar in Her Majesty's Courts of Law or Equity in Ontario unless he has been entered and admitted into the Law Society, under its rules, as a Barrister.

The Lieutenant-Governor by letters patent under the Great Seal of the Province may appoint from among the members of the Bar Provincial Officers under the name of Her Majesty's Counsel learned in the Law. usually

called Queen's Counsel, who are entitled to hold
Court at Assize or *nisi prius* at the request of
the presiding Judge or otherwise; and have
certain other rights and privileges as to procedure in Court, &c.*

The Attorney-General for the Dominion ranks
first in precedence in the Ontario Bar, then the
Attorney-General for the Province, then previous
Attorney-Generals according to seniority of appointment.   After these Solicitor-Generals and
such Queen's Counsel as were appointed before
Confederation, in the same order.   Other members rank in the order of the call to the Bar.

Attorneys and Solicitors are admitted into
the Law Society under rules somewhat similar
as to Barristers, and must not practice without paying an annual fee and obtaining a cert'fi-
cate.   They may be struck off the Roll of any of
the Courts by a Superior Court Judge on application being made in a proper case.   It is usual
to speak of members of the Legal profession as
Attorneys when conducting actions or suits in
the Common Law Courts, and Solicitors in the
Chancery or Insolvency Courts.   In the Maritime Court they are styled Proctors.   The profession of Barrister in Ontario, though not so
distinct as in England from the office of Solicitor or Attorney, is yet separate from the latter.
Generally Barristers here are members of both

---

* In Lenoir *vs.* Ritchie, several of the Judges in the Supreme Court
held that the Local Legislatures have no power to pass an Act authorizing the appointment of Queen's Counsel.

professions—if indeed there can be said to be two professions in the Province. A number of Solicitors, however, are not Barristers, and therefore not entitled to plead in Court. On the other hand, a Barrister who is not an Attorney or Solicitor as well, is not privileged to act in any other capacity than that of arguing in Court the cases which the Attorneys or Solicitors prepare for him.

The Judges of the Superior Courts are selected from Barristers of at least ten years standing. In other Courts the length of time varies with the Court.

In Quebec all Advocates, Barristers, Attorneys, Solicitors and Proctors-at-Law, form a Corporation called *The Bar of Lower Canada.* A certain number of officers of each of the sections into which the Corporation is divided constitutes a Council with powers somewhat analogous to the Law Society of Upper Canada.

They entertain matters, however, among the members of the profession not dealt with in Ontario by the Law Society, noticeably the pronouncing of censures for any breach of discipline or action derogatory to the honor of the Bar through the *Bâtonnier.* Members may be suspended by this officer, subject to approval of the Council. In the two Provinces also there is a great difference as regards NOTARIES PUBLIC. In Quebec these form a separate profession, being divided into a number of bodies corporate under

Acts very similar to those relating to the Bar of the Province. Their duties not only embrace the certifying and protesting of documents, but includes nearly all of what is understood in English practice by conveyancing.

In Ontario a Notary Public is appointed by the Lieutenant-Governor, and may protest Bills of Exchange and Promissory Notes ; and may draw, pass, keep and issue all deeds and contracts, charter parties, and other mercantile transactions in this Province, may give certificates as to copies of instruments, and has some other undefined duties. They form no profession and are part of none, though the Commission is usually granted to members of the legal profession as of course.

Any person not a Barrister or Attorney must, however, pass an examination as to his qualification for the office before his County Judge, or before some one appointed for that purpose by the Lieutenant-Governor, and produce a certificate that on examination he is found qualified for the office ; and further, that in the examiner's opinion a Notary Public is needed in the place where the applicant intends to carry on business. Under certain Statutes they can administer oaths or affirmations, though usually the Courts of Queen's Bench and Common Pleas appoint Commissioners for taking affidavits for this purpose, who have power within the County in which they reside.

The Sheriff is an officer of the Courts appointed by the Lieutenant-Governor under the Great Seal, one for each county, and holds office during pleasure. This office is one of the oldest and most honorable in the gift of the Crown. Formerly he held a Court for his shire or county, and the word Sheriff means a *Reeve* of the *Shire*. He attended the King's Court and looked after the peace of the county. He is yet the Chief Executive Officer of the Courts, attends the Judge in circuit, summons the juries, has charge of the gaols, and executes all writs and sentences of the Courts up to the extreme penalty of the law. Where the Sheriff is personally interested in a case, or where he cannot or will not execute the process of the Court, the writs may be addressed to the principal Coroner of the county.

CHAPTER XLIV.

BRITISH COLONIAL COURT

THE JUDICIAL COMMITTEE OF THE PRIVY COUNCIL.

THIS Court is the last resort of a Colonial British subject in appeal from the laws of his own Colony.

The Privy Council in England is composed of a large number of distinguished persons. Most of the principal Judges, the Speaker of the House of Commons, the Queen's Ambassadors and those formerly holding offices in the Ministry, besides the Archbishops and some Bishops, are members of this body. One distinguished Committee forms the Cabinet; another, with which only we have to deal with here, forms a Judicial Committee; and its functions are to decide all matters that can judicially come by appeal or by complaint in the nature of appeal before the Queen, or the Queen in Council. On hearing the case argued this Committee report to the Queen in Council their recommendation for her decision.

This Court is composed of such Privy Councillors as are or were its presidents, Judges of the Chief Courts of Equity and Common Law, the Judges of the Admiralty, of the Prerogative Court of Canterbury, Bishops and Archbishops, two retired East Indian or Colonial Judges, and two others. *

* Cox's British Commonwealth.

The Committee has the ordinary powers of the Superior Courts in England as to witnesses, juries, process, &c. ; and cases may be heard by three of its members and the Lord President. The Court holds three sittings in the year. generally in February, June and November, lasting usually six weeks.

The jurisdiction of the Judicial Committee is divided into two heads—one being where an appeal is allowed by right and the other where leave to appeal is first of all necessary. The Crown may, in Acts of its Colonial Legislatures, shut out the right to appeal—it may abrogate its perogative. Where the right of the Crown is not reserved, or where the fair construction of the Colonial Act is that no appeal will be to the Privy Council, then the judgment of a Colonial Court under the provisions of such an Act, which was assented to by the Crown, is final. The Crown, by assenting, takes away the right of appeal.

In the Quebec Controverted Elections Act of 1875, the Act states that the judgment of the Court " shall not be susceptible of Appeal ;" and an appeal to the Privy Council was refused in a case coming under this Act.*

The Canadian Act establishing the Supreme Court at Ottawa in 1875, made its judgments final without appeal, saving any right which Her Majesty may exercise in virtue of the Royal prerogative.

---

* Theberge *vs.* Landry, 2 App. Cas. 102.

Lord Cairns, in construing the Section of the Supreme Court Act containing these words, lays it down that the Judicial Committee of the Privy Council would have no hesitation in a proper case of advising Her Majesty to allow an appeal upon the judgment of this Court.

The discretion of so allowing an appeal to be heard would not be exercised where the amount involved was small, and where the issue between the treaties related simply to the legal construction of a particular contract, or where no general principle was involved, or where no other cases were necessarily affected by the decision complained of.*

Appeals lie as a matter of right from the Provinces.

So far as Colonial cases are concerned it is said that no appeal lies in any case of felony.

When the last Court is reached in criminal matters the condemned has the right to sue for pardon at the foot of the throne. Formerly the pardoning power was supposed to be or was in reality in the personal discretion of the Governor-General.

The instructions as to pardon are now to this effect :

"The Governor-General is not to pardon or reprieve any offender who may be tried within the Dominion without first receiving in Capital cases the advice of the Privy Council, and in other cases the advice of at least

---

* Johnston *vs.* The Minister and Trustees of St. Andrew's Church, Montreal, 3 App. Cas. 159.

one minister. And in cases in which such pardon or reprieve might directly affect the interests of the Empire, or of any country or place beyond the jurisdiction of the Government of the Dominion, the said Governor-General shall, before deciding as to either pardon or reprieve, take these interests specially into his own personal consideration in conjunction with such advice as afore. said."*

Appeals to Her Majesty in Her Privy Council are entertained from the Court of Appeal in Ontario, where the matter in controversy exceeds the sum or value of $4,000, and in cases relating to the taking of any annual or other rent, customary or other duty or fee, or any like demand of a general or public nature affecting future rights, no matter what the amount in question may be. Beyond these no appeals lie from the Court of Appeal in Ontario to the Judicial Committee of the Privy Council.

Security to the amount of $2,000 must be given in these cases.

All cases of Appeal are commenced by Petition addressed to Her Majesty in Council; and this is the first step in their prosecution. Afterwards certified copies of the record from the Court appealed from are sent to England and deposited in the Council office; and an appearance having been entered by the respondent, each side makes up its own case if it is allowed to be heard.

Earl Carnarvon, in 1874, intimated to the Governor-General of Canada that in order to

---

* Instructions to His Excellency the Marquis of Lorne.

bring Appeals from the Supreme Court of Canada, a Petition for that purpose should be brought before the Judicial Committee of the Privy Council, and not transmitted through the Secretary of State to the Queen in Council, in order to obtain leave to appeal. He also intimated as the practice that the Petitioner must enter an appearance before any answer is returned by the Judicial Committee in answer to the Petition. The Governor-General hereafter is to decline transmitting applications in a private suit to the Secretary of State for the Colonies, but is to inform the Petitioner what steps to take in the matter. The circular dispatch of Earl Carnarvon, though directed to the practice in appeals, is an indication that the Royal Prerogative as to allowing them from Canada would. be exercised in the recommendation of the Judicial Committee itself. In effect it would seem to be similar to an application to any appellate court for leave to appeal, where such leave is necessary.

The Judicial Committee has unlimited powers in the way of procedure, and takes no notice of the rules in the Court below as binding upon it.

The case is argued by senior and junior Counsel, the appellant's Counsel having the right to reply.

The judgment of the Court is delivered by one Judge only, and need not be unanimous, a majority being sufficient.*

---

* Lattey's Privy Council Practice.

A question has been lately discussed in England whether a dissenting member of the Committee could declare his dissent. A great deal of learning and historical research were expended on another question out of which this arose. that is, whether or not the Judicial Committee of the Privy Council is a *Court* at all, or merely a *consultative* body. If a Court, then each member would have the right to express a dissenting opinion or judgment; and if the usages and traditions of the Privy Councils were to govern, then there could be no dissent. at least in expression.*

The Judgment, after being delivered, is reported to the Committee, and submitted to the Queen in Council for approval. The order made thereupon is the last proceeding in the case, and the Judicial rights of the parties determined.

* See Finlayson's History of the Judicial Committee of the Privy Council.

CHAPTER XLV.

THE SUPREME COURT OF CANADA.

THIS Court is the highest Court of Appeal within Canada, and entertains appeals within and throughout the Dominion from the last Court of resort in the Provinces. By leave, however, it may hear an appeal from any decree, decretal, or order made by a Court of Equity, or in an Equity proceeding or any final judgment of the Superior Courts, other than those of Quebec, without intermediate appeal to such last Provincial Court, providing the case originally commenced in such Superior Court. In certain cases in election petitions an appeal in the same way will lie to this Court. In Equity cases, and in proceedings in the nature of equity, an appeal will lie to this Court, even from orders made in the exercise of Judicial discretion.

The intention of the Act establishing the Supreme and Exchequer Courts is that all orders, decretal orders, decrees and decisions of any Superior Court made in any such cause, matter or other judicial proceeding in Equity, or in any action, cause, suit, matter or other judicial proceeding in the nature of a suit or proceeding in Equity, are and always have been proper subjects of appeal to this Court.

In Quebec cases, the appeal must always come from the Court of Queen's Bench ; and the matter in controversy must be at least $2,000, unless it involves the validity of a Dominion or Local Act of the Legislature or of any Act or Ordinance of the Territories or districts of Canada, or any fee of office, duty, rent, revenue, or any sum of money payable to Her Majesty or any title to lands or tenements, or annual rents, if brought in the Court mentioned.

The Court has jurisdiction in criminal as well as in civil matters ; but in respect of treason, felony and misdemeanor, no appeal is allowed if the judgment of the Lower Court was unanimous in affirming the convictions.

This Court of last resort does not mean the individual judges who may be authorized to sit in these Courts, but the tribunals from which the appeals are to come, or the respective Courts themselves, without reference to the number of Judges, provided always the Court be duly constituted by the presence of a sufficient number of Judges to make a legal court, whatever that number may be.* The judgment of two or even of one Judge where the Court may be constituted of that number respectively is not appealable. An appeal lies only where there is a dissenting judgment in the Court appealed from.†

* Per Mr. Justice (now Chief Justice) Ritchie in Amer *vs.* The Queen, 2 S. C.

† Mr. Justice Taschereau in the same case.

14

No appeal lies to this Court from the judgment of a Court granting a new trial on the ground that the verdict was against the weight of evidence, that being a matter of discretion.*

The Governor-General may refer any matter to the Supreme Court for hearing or consideration, and they shall certify their opinion thereon to the Governor in Council; and either House of Parliament may refer any private Bill or Petition thereto.

Controversies arising between the Dominion and the Provinces, or between the Provinces themselves, may, with the consent of the Provinces, be determined by the Supreme or the Exchequer Court of Canada. The Province of Ontario has placed herself within this jurisdiction by enacting that the Supreme Court may entertain controversies between the Dominion and the Provinces, and also controversies between Ontario and any other Province submitting to the jurisdiction of the Court. In such actions and proceedings in Ontario, where the parties thereto by their pleadings raised the question of the validity of any Dominion or Provincial Act, if in the opinion of the Judge the question is material, the case may be ordered by the Judge, either with or without the request of the parties, to be removed to the Supreme Court.

The Court, or any of its Judges, has original jurisdictions in *habeas corpus* cases; and has the

---

* Boak *vs.* The Merchant's Marine Insurance Co'y. 1 S. C.

same power to bail, discharge or commit the prisoner as any Court or Judge in the Provinces having jurisdiction in such matters.

The Court, or any Judge, may also order the issue of a writ of *Certiorari* to bring up papers or proceedings necessary with a view to any enquiry, appeal or other proceeding before such Court or Judge.

The Supreme Court sits three times a year, on the third Tuesday of February, the first Tuesday in May, and the fourth Tuesday in October, at Ottawa, and is presided over by a Chief Justice and five Associate Judges, who hold office during good behaviour. Any five of the Judges are competent to hold Court in term. The Judges are incapable of holding any office of emolument under the Dominion or Provincial Governments.

Rules in relation to appeals are laid down by Order in Council, and the Judges of the Court can make rules and orders for the purposes of carrying out the Acts establishing this Court.

All Barristers or Advocates, Attorneys or Solicitors, in any of the Provinces shall have the right to practice as Barristers, Advocates, Solicitors, &c., and Counsel in this and in the Exchequer Court ; and all such practitioners are officers of these Courts.

A Registrar and Reporter of the Court are appointed by the Governor in Council.

The proceedings in this Court are regulated by rules approved of by the Court.

The first proceeding in appeals is the filing of a case stated by the parties setting forth the judgment objected to and so much of the pleadings, evidence, affidavits, and documents as may be necessary to raise the question for the decision of the Court. The case must also, if possible, contain a transcript of all the opinions or reasons delivered by the Judges in the Courts below, and must be accompanied by a certificate that proper security to the extent of $500 has been given by the appellant in the Court appealed from.

Twenty-five copies of the case are printed in a prescribed form ; and these, with certified copies of original documents, deposited with the Registrar of the Court. Notice of hearing is served at least a month before the next session of the Court, at which time each party deposits in Court copies of the *factum* or points for argument in appeal. This contains a concise statement of facts, the points of law and the arguments and authorities in the case, and is printed and distributed the same as the case or appeal. These are put in under seal ; and, when deposited, are exchanged with the opposite party. When the rules of Court are complied with the appeals are set down for hearing, and the case is heard with not more than two Counsel for each side—one only in reply. These rules do not apply to criminal appeals or to *habeas corpus* cases, in which a certified written case is all that is necessary in order to bring them before the Court.

In election appeals, the record or the necessary part of it, is printed under the direction of the Registrar of the Court, but each *factum* is prepared the same as in ordinary cases.

A tariff of costs has been drawn up by the judges; and the Court has full power as to execution to enforce its orders.

THE only other Dominion Court is the Exchequer Court of Canada.

This Court looks after the Revenue of the country, enforces certain penalties on behalf of the Crown, and has jurisdiction in all cases in which demand shall be made or relief sought in respect of any matter which might in England be the subject of a suit or action in the Court of Exchequer on its plea side against any officer of the Crown. It also deals exclusively with those cases which, in the English Exchequer Court, were instituted on its revenue side against the Crown.

The Exchequer Courts can hear appeals in all cases of arbitration arising under the Acts respecting the Public Works of Canada when the claim is over $500. In all cases the submission of the parties as to arbitration can be made a rule of this Court; and the Court has full power over any award—to set it aside or remit the matters referred for re-consideration—and may make final order as to what it deems just and right between the parties.

An appeal lies to the Supreme Court in these cases.

The Supreme Court Judges are the Judges of this Court; and the practice and procedure are laid down in very elaborate rules framed by all the Judges of the Supreme Court.

Cases are heard before a single Judge in the first instance with or without a jury, and an appeal lies to the Supreme Court.

The Court sits at any place in Canada, and the Sheriffs and Coroners of the different Counties are officers of this Court also. In Ontario a Judge of the Exchequer Court has, in regard to the use of the Court House and other buildings set apart in the County for the administration of Justice, the same authority in all respects as a Judge at *Nisi Prius.*

Execution can issue out of this Court, both to enforce its own decrees and those of the Supreme Court, the writs issuing in the name of the Chief Justice of the Supreme Court.

The Registrar of the Supreme Court is appointed for this Court also; and all Barristers, Attorneys, etc., are officers of the Court, the same as in the Supreme Court of Canada.

CHAPTER XLVII

CRIMINAL LAW.

THE Procedure in Criminal Law is directed by Acts of the Dominion Parliament, and is almost uniformly the same in all the Provinces.

In criminal trials, as it is the public that is wronged, the action is said to be brought by the Queen or King against the accused. The case under our Statutes is commenced either on information laid before a Justice of the Peace, or Police Magistrate, the inquistion of a Coroner's jury or the presentment of a grand jury.

When an indictable offence is laid before a Justice of the Peace, if the evidence is sufficient to put the accused on his trial, the Justice must either send him to gaol to await the next sitting of the Court or admit him to bail. The evidence and information are transmitted to the County Crown Attorney, who takes up the case on behalf of the Crown, after the Justice of the Peace or Magistrate has disposed of his share of it. This is the usual way in which criminal trials are begun.

It is true that on leave being obtained a criminal information may be filed in the Court of Queen's Bench in Ontario; but this is rarely done, and is the only case where proceedings are begun in a high Court of Justice. No criminal information will lie in regard to a felony or high treason. The procedure only applies to those misdemeanors upon which an indictment would lie before a Justice of the Peace. Leave to file a criminal information rests in the discretion of the Court, and is a proceeding of an extraordinary character in criminal matters. In England it is granted when the matter complained of is of public importance, and that a speedy remedy is desired and necessary, or where some important or superior person is the subject of grave charges; but the tendency of the Courts here would seem to be to discourage the practice of granting leave for such informations.

A number of cases are also sent up to the County Crown Attorney from the Coroners of the different Counties.

In cases where manslaughter or murder has been committed, the Coroner empannels a jury, and their verdict or inquest is transmitted to the Crown Attorney as in the case of Justices' committals. The County Attorney attends with these informations and inquisitions at the next sitting of the Court of competent jurisdiction and prefers them to the Grand Jury for their opinion as to whether or not the evidence is sufficient to put the accused on his trial.

A Grand Jury is comprised of not less than twelve or not more than twenty-three persons selected to be Grand Jurors; and their duty is to judge whether the prisoner ought to be put on his trial or not.

In certain cases, such as perjury, suborna-
tion of perjury, conspiracy, obtaining money
or other property by false pretences, keeping a
gambling house, keeping a disorderly house, or
any indecent assault, no presentment to or finding by the Grand Jury is made without the person making the accusation first giving a bond
to prosecute or give evidence in the matter;
unless the accused is committed, or in custody,
or that the indictment is preferred by the Attorney or Solicitor-General of the Province, or by a
Judge competent to give such a direction or try
the offence.

The Grand Jury judge nothing of the guilt or
innocence of the accused ; that is left to another
jury. In the finding which the Grand Jury
makes to the presiding Judge, if in their
opinion the accused ought to be put on his trial
they write " true bill" on the back of the information or inquisition ; and if not they write " no
bill" and the accused is dicharged without trial.

The Grand Jury also presents a statement in
reference to the state of the County Jails,
Asylums, &c., which is called a presentment, and
in this they can take notice of certain crimes and
have the accused put on his trial.

After the Grand Jury brings in a true bill the
accused pleads guilty or not guilty ; or in the
event of his silence, the Court can plead not
guilty for him.

In capital offences the accused can object to
or challenge not more than twenty jurors. In

other cases of felony not more than twelve jurors, and in all other cases four jurors. These may be objected to without any reason given. Any number may be objected to on cause assigned. The Crown has the right to challenge four jurors peremptorily, and has also the right to cause any juror to stand aside until the panel has been gone through, and has the same rights as the accused as to challenge for cause.

The accused, after the close of the case for the Crown, can make full answer and defence to any indictment preferred against him, and be heard by his Counsel on his behalf.

The presiding Judge, on the finding of the jury, sentences the accused or discharges him as the case may be. From this there is no appeal. The Judge may reserve any question of Law to any of the Superior Courts of Common Law. But in case the Judge refuses to reserve a point of Law, or could not have reserved it, a writ of error may issue so as to bring the matter under the consideration of Superior Courts of Law. If the conviction is bad for any cause, the whole trial is a nullity, and a new trial may be granted in such cases. In the absence of reprieve or pardon by the Crown the sentence of the law is carried out by the various punishments of death, imprisonment, &c., provided by the Statutes in that behalf.

The appeals to the Supreme Court, as well as the exercise of pardon, have been adverted to heretofore.

CHAPTER XLVIII

JUSTICES OF THE PEACE.

ONE of the Prerogatives of the Crown is, that the King or Queen is the fountain of Justice. In view of this the Sovereign has charge of the peace of the realm ; and in order that peace should prevail, certain magistrates, called Justices of the Peace, are appointed by commission from the Queen. In Ontario these commissions come through the Lieutenant-Governor in Council through the Clerk of the Peace for each County, and only the most sufficient persons are chosen for the office.

Certain other persons, from the nature of the offices they hold, are also Justices of the Peace, such as Mayors of Cities and Towns, Aldermen who have qualified themselves for that purpose, and the Reeves and Deputy Reeves of Township and Village Corporations. The Judges of the Supreme and Exchequer Courts of Canada, and the Justices of the Court of Appeal and of the Courts of Queen's Bench and Common Pleas and of the Court of Chancery for Ontario, are Justices for the whole of this Province. The Judges of the County Courts are also Justices of the Peace ; and it would appear that the members of the Executive Council for this Province, the

Attorney-General for the Dominion and the Provinces, and in certain cases Queen's Counsel, are also Justices of the Peace by virtue of their office or position.

Where Justices of the Peace are appointed by commission by the Lieutenant-Governor they must have, besides the mental qualifications necessary for the importance of the office, some interest in land to the value of at least $1,200. Unless where specially provided for, no Attorney or Solicitor, while practicing as such, shall be a Justice of the Peace; and no Sheriff or Coroner, acting as such, shall be qualified for this position. Every Justice of the Peace must take a prescribed oath before fulfilling any of the duties of his office.

The authority under which they act is called their Commission, and was settled by all the Judges in England over five hundred years ago; so that the office is a very ancient as well as a very honourable one.

Each ordinary Justice of the Peace has a certain district or territory within which his jurisdiction lies; beyond that he has no power. The duties of a Justice of the Peace are of two kinds: 1st, Judicial duties; and 2nd, Ministerial duties. When any person prefers a charge against another before a Justice of the Peace, the latter may issue a summons or a warrant to apprehend the offender; the summons being a command to the offender to appear on a certain day, and is

for trifling matters or disputes—the warrant
being for all serious offences, and is the Constable's authority for arresting and keeping the
accused in his charge till brought before the
Justice of the Peace. If the summons be dis-
obeyed, the Justice may issue a warrant to apprehend the offender.

The Justice may require in all cases that the
person preferring a charge against another
should make his statement on oath. In the
cases of perjury, &c., where a bond conditioned
on the prosecution and giving evidence is
necessary before a Bill of Indictment should be
presented to, or found by, a Grand Jury, as mentioned in the last chapter, a prosecutor desiring
to prefer an indictment respecting any of these
offences before one or more Justices of the Peace
having jurisdiction in the matter, and who may
refuse to commit or bail the person accused,
must give his bond or recognizance to the Justice
or Justices that he will prosecute the charge or
complaint ; and thereupon the Justice or Justices
must transmit the recognizance, information and
depositions, if any, to the proper officer in the
same way as if the accused had been committed.

Where a felony or misdemeanor has been
committed the charge in the affidavit is called
an information and a warrant issued. On the
accused appearing before the Justice, witnesses
are examined and the proceedings conducted with
the regularity of a Court.

In serious cases where an indictment would lie against the accused, the statement of the accused is taken down, read over to him, and signed by him in the presence of the Justice, and also signed by the Justice himself. When all the evidence is taken, and the case argued by Counsel, when such is necessary or permitted, the Justice decides on the case.

If it is an offence for which the law has given the Justice express power by Statute to impose a fine or imprison the accused, and that there is sufficient evidence to warrant fine or imprisonment, then the Justice summarily convicts the accused. This is called a Summary Conviction, and is regulated by Act of Parliament.

In these cases, if the evidence be insufficient to warrant a summary conviction, or if the Justice had no authority to convict, or if for other good reasons the conviction be bad, the Superior Courts of Law, on application being made by the accused, will quash the conviction by *Certiorari*. An appeal lies to the County Judge and to the Court of General Sessions from the conviction of a Justice of the Peace.

At the hearing of any appeal under the Act relating to summary convictions, any of the parties to the appeal may call witnesses and adduce evidence, who or which may not have been called or adduced at the original hearing.

No action will lie against a Justice of the Peace acting within his jurisdiction in the discharge of his duty unless he acted maliciously and without reasonable or probable cause; and no action can be brought against a Justice of the Peace except within six months after judgment. In all such cases of summary conviction a Justice of the Peace acts judicially.

But a Justice of the Peace has Ministerial duties to perform as well as Judicial ones. After hearing all the evidence in a case before him there may be sufficient to justify him in finding the accused guilty of some crime over which the Justice has no power or authority to convict summarily. It may be for a crime of a serious nature, such as murder, manslaughter, or some indictable offence and over these a Justice of the Peace has no power. There are certain offences in which, if the accused consents, a Justice of the Peace or Police Magistrate may try the case and sentence the accused to such punishment as may be determined by the Statutes in that behalf. But without such consent, punishment would not be inflicted. The accused is not deprived of the benefit of a jury of his countrymen as to whether or not he is guilty of the crime charged against him.

An indictment, it will be remembered, is the test of a crime, and the evidence must be considered by a Grand Jury to be sufficient to put the accused on his trial. As the law at present stands the judgment of two Justices of the Peace is supplanted by that of a Grand Jury, on the sufficiency of the evidence to support an indict-ment. On the duties of the Justice on an indictable offence being brought under his notice, they are so far judicial that in a proper case he can admit the accused to bail till the next sittings of the Court. No Justices shall admit to bail any one charged with treason or a capital offence; but any two Justices may bail parties charged with other felonies. Where the offence is not bailable by him his duties are purely ministerial. If the evidence supports the charge the accused must be committed to gaol. The depositions and prisoner's statement are sent to the County Attorney, and the case tried either at the County Judge's Criminal Court, the Court of General Sessions, or the Court of Oyer and Terminer and General Gaol Delivery. In the two latter Courts the accused has a jury to find whether the evidence points to his guilt; in the County Judge's Criminal Court the accused can elect to be tried without a jury. This only refers to offences for which the accused can be tried at the General Sessions.

So far as summary convictions are concerned the Magistrate's decision is final, unless set aside on appeal on application to quash the same. But all committals, after being disposed of by him, are tried in the Courts as already mentioned. If the Justice refuses to bail the person an applica-tion, even in cases of murder, can be made to the Superior Courts of law; and if a proper case be made to the satisfaction of the Judge, bail can be put in for his appearance.

In cases of felony one Justice cannot dispose of the case, it requires two at least ; but a Police Magistrate, County Judge, or Stipendiary Magistrate may of himself do whatever is authorized by our Criminal law to be done by two or more Justices of the Peace. Justices of the Peace are aided and attended by constables, whose duties are to execute the commands of the Justices. They may commit an offender and convey him to prison if the offence was done in their presence, but have no authority to arrest a man for an affray done out of their presence. Each Justice appoints his own constables ; and when necessary any two or more Justices can appoint special constables upon the oath of a credible witness that any tumult, riot, or felony has taken place, or is continuing, or is to be expected to take place. A County Constable is appointed by the County Judge, or by the Court of General Sessions, and the Lieutenant-Governor may appoint one for the whole Province.

In Cities and Towns with a population of over 5,000 inhabitants, instead of Justices of the Peace, a Police Magistrate is appointed, who has generally the same powers as two or more Justices would have, and may entertain cases requiring more than one Justice of the Peace. The Police force in the city or town attend and execute his commands, much the same as Constables do with those of Justices of the Peace. Such Police Magistrate holds office during pleasure; and by virtue of his appointment as such, is a Justice of the Peace for the city or town where he is appointed. Every other Justice of the Peace within the city or town where a Police Magistrate has been appointed ceases to have any powers to admit to bail or discharge any person, or act in any way within the Judicial limits of the city or town, except at the request of the Police Magistrate, or during his illness or absence.

Every other Justice of the Peace, however, is liable to act as one of the Justices of the Courts of General Sessions. A Police Magistrate so appointed, besides having the powers of two or more Justices of the Peace as to matters within the Legislative control of this Province, has jurisdiction over all prosecutions for offences against the City or Town by-laws, and penalties as to refusing to accept offices therein, or to make the necessary declarations of qualification and office.

CHAPTER XLIX.

CORONERS.

CORONERS are also conservators of the peace, and are said to be the only officers known to the English law charged with the investigation of crime. They are called Coroners from *corona*, the Latin word for Crown, because formerly they attended to the pleas of the Crown. Their duties at present are mostly defined by Statute law; and with the exception of acting at times in place of the Sheriff of their county, are limited to inquisitions on deceased persons and as to the origin of fires.

Coroners are appointed by the Lieutenant-Governor under the Great Seal; one or more Coroners for each County, City, Town or District in the Province; and hold office for life, unless they are removed for improper conduct or resign their Commission. It may be that besides those appointed in this way that the Chief Justices of the Court of Queen's Bench and Common Pleas are Coroners for the whole Province, in analogy to the English doctrine, that the Lord Chief Justice of the Queen's Bench is the supreme Coroner in the land.

The office of Coroner, like that of Sheriff, is very ancient and very honorable. The Peace of the County in England was entrusted to these two officers when the Earls gave up the ward-ship of the County. It thus happened that the Coroner often fulfilled the duties of the Sheriff; and such is the practice to this day; so that whenever the Sheriff has an interest in the suit, or makes default in serving process, the writs are directed to the Coroner.

This is part of the Ministerial function of a Coroner; and besides acting as Sheriff's substitute, they can arrest persons committing an affray in their presence; and they possibly possess other magisterial powers.

But the Judicial functions of a Coroner are what must be considered as properly coming under Criminal law. Whenever it has been made to appear to a Coroner that there is reason to believe that a deceased person came to his death, through violence or unfair means, or by culpable or negligent conduct of himself or others, under such circumstances as require investigation, and not through mere accident or mischance, he is to direct an inquest to be held on the body of such deceased person.

On the death of any person in any Gaol, Prison, House of Correction, Lock-up House, or House of Industry, no matter from what cause, an inquest is to be held, as the Crown desires to see that the inmates of these places are properly taken care of and do not die of want, or from improper treatment from the custodians or otherwise. In furtherance of this, notice must

be given immediately to the Coroner of the death
of the prisoner.

In all cases the inquest is held upon view of the
body ; and the investigation extends to the cause
of the death of the person, and to an enquiry of
those accessories who it appeared were absent at
the time the offence, if chargeable against any
one, was committed, but who procured, counseled,
commanded or abetted it.   In other words, it
extends to principals in the crime and accessories before the fact.

To aid him in this investigation the Coroner
issues a warrant to summon a Jury at a certain
time, not being a Sunday, and at a place
named in the warrant.   A Constable summons
the Jury, at least twelve in number ; and it
appears that no one is exempt from serving
thereon, and may be fined for non-attendance.

Witnesses can be summoned at the same time,
and are examined after the Coroner's Court is
opened and the Jury sworn.   The accused can
have his witnesses in his own favor ; and after all
the evidence is heard the Coroner sums it up to
the Jury, explains to them what the law is on the
subject, and directs them to consider of their
verdict—they are judges of what the facts are.
A unanimous verdict of twelve is required ; and if
it is a case to come up at the Assizes the
witnesses may be bound to appear at the trial to
give evidence, and the prosecutor to appear and
prosecute.

A written statement of the finding of the jury or their verdict is called an Inquisition; and when it contains the subject matter of accusation it need not come before a Grand Jury at the Assizes, as the information of a Magistrate or of Justices of the Peace must. The principle in English law, that no man is to be deprived of his life unless on the unanimous verdict of twenty-four, is still regarded, the only difference being that the Grand Jury in this case is superseded by a Coroner's Jury. The party accused, if the crime charged be murder, or an accessory to murder before the fact, or manslaughter, is to be apprehended and committed to jail, but may apply to a Judge of one of the Superior Courts for bail, if so advised.

The Inquisition itself may be quashed if taken before an unauthorized person, or if the Coroner or Jury misconducted themselves, or for other good causes; but any technical defect or omission, of any matter unnecessary to be proved, will not vitiate any inquisition. Every Coroner, immediately after inquisition found by him, shall return the same, and all papers in reference thereto and to the attendance of witnesses, to the County Crown Attorney.

Coroners also enquire into the origin of fires, where there is reason to believe the fire was the result of culpable or negligent conduct or design, or occurred under such circumstances as require investigation. The Coroner can in his discretion empannel a jury or not, unless he is required to do so in the written requisition of an Insurance Agent, or of any three householders living near the fire. The inquest is conducted the same as an any ordinary inquest on the body of a deceased person ; but the return is made to the Clerk of the Peace instead of to the County Crown Attorney. With the exception, however, of the County of York, the Clerk of the Peace is the same person as the County Crown Attorney in Ontario.

Each Coroner, before the first day of January in each year, makes a return to the Provincial Treasurer of the list of inquests taken before him. The Informations of Justices of the Peace and the Inquisitions of Coroners, as was seen, are both returned to the same officer, the Crown Attorney for the County. He is therefore the next officer immediately concerned in the administration of Criminal Justice.

THE COUNTY CROWN ATTORNEY.

THE Lieutenant-Governor appoints a Crown Attorney for each County in the Province, who holds office during pleasure. In Ontario he must be a resident in the County and a Barrister of at least three years standing. He is incapacitated, either directly or indirectly, to act as counsel for any prisoner charged with treason, felony or other offence punishable under the criminal law in force. His duties are laid down by statute, and refer almost, if not altogether, to criminal matters. It is his duty to receive and examine informations, examinations, and inquisitions, and all papers connected with criminal charges which the Justices of the Peace and the Coroners of his County are required to transmit to him.

He secures the attendance of witnesses; institutes and conducts on the part of the Crown all the criminal business at the Court of General Sessions and the County Judge's Criminal Court. He advises Justices of the Peace upon being asked to do so ; and has certain duties as to the Public Revenue, Public Health, or any matter punishable by a Justice of the Peace. In Criminal cases at the Assizes, such as for felonies and treasons, he is required to be present and assist the Crown Counsel; and in his absence, to take charge of the Criminal business of the Court.

CHAPTER LI.

CONCLUSION.

In a work intended to describe the present Constitution, it is probably no part of the writer's duty to find fault with the existing state of things, or suggest changes in the system of Government that obtains amongst us.

It is an undeniable fact, however, that Canada, with a population somewhat exceeding that of the city of London, has a system of Governments as elaborate as that of the United States for its population of ten times that number. We have a central Government with powers largely in advance, comparatively speaking, of that at Washington; and we have Provincial Governments which, even if their limits are narrowly hedged in, are yet each year asserting the necessity of their existence by volumes of statutory enactments. If these enactments be all necessary, and it must be assumed that they are, the central Government might sit at Ottawa all the year through and not do one-half of it at all—and probably not do a tenth of it efficiently. A House full of such members is poor machinery for legislating on any subjects; but totally inadequate for the local concerns of remote Provinces. The Provinces are too scattered and their interests too diverse to admit of the possibility of legislating for all by the ordinary means of two Houses of Parliament. The members may understand the legislation proposed or needed for their own Provinces: but they would neither know nor understand, and probably would'nt care, about the legislation needed a thousand miles off.

Canada, considered in point of territory, has a good deal of similarity to the United States; and it cannot be said that in copying the Constitution of that country to the extent that she has done, any mistake was committed. Local concerns in a large country are managed most satisfactorily by Local Administration; and it wont matter any whether such Administration is a District Council or a Parliament. It may be matter of importance if the cost of sustaining one form is much more expensive than the other.

In our Provinces the people pay a high price for their Government; but it is the sort of Government they wanted; and it is to be hoped that they get the worth of their money. It is cheaper in the long run than unsatisfactory Government at a lower figure.

A little consideration will show that the people of the Dominion cannot be legislated for in the same way as five or six millions of people may be in a thickly settled or confined district. There is a strip of the broadest part of the Continent extending from ocean to ocean. There are different modes of life among its inhabitants—in

Nova Scotia, in Manitoba, in British Columbia—
each requiring special local legislation ; different
customs, races and religions even in the twin Provinces of Ontario and Quebec—different features
everywhere.

The Provinces may be governed by the ordinary machinery of two Houses, but not governed
so satisfactorily as at present.   There has been
ample experience to shew this in the past history
of any two of them.

The numerous Legislatures that obtain amongst
us must, therefore, in view of these facts, be
regarded as things of necessity.   The misfortune
is that we have not population to justify such an
array.   It is some consolation, however, that
when our Provinces and Territories number a
great many millions more than they do at
present, the Constitution of 1867 will have sup-
plied abundant machinery to govern them without
many additions to its provisions.

INDEX.

Functions, Judicial, by whom exercised, 4.
Fund, the Consolidated Revenue, origin of, 115 ; what
    composes the, 115 ; how augmented, 117 ; charges
    on, 118.
Government, what is the, 3 ; to whom entrusted, 3 ; the
    three functions of, 4 ; in whom reposed under
    Quebec Act, 8 ; under Constitutional Act, 9 ; under
    Union Act, 12 ; place of sitting, 12 ; form of, from
    1760–1867, 13 ; contrast between Canadian and
    United States, 17 ; principles of, 18 ; for what
    answerable, 74 ; who may be a member of, 74 ; when
    harmony required from members of, 76.
Government, Administrative, what is, 74.
Government, Colonial, in Canada, first steps taken
    towards, 8.
Government, Constitutional, see Government Respon-
    sible.
Government, Executive, division of, 79 ; in whom
    vested, 79.
Government, Provincial, what generally composes, 16.
Government, Responsible, what is, 4.
Governor in Council, controlling power of, over Provin-
    cial Legislature, 131.
Governor General, functions and prerogatives of, 25, 33,
    79 ; may reserve Bills for Queen's assent, 27 ; effect
    of refusing assent to a Bill passed by both Houses,
    28 ; by whom appointed, 31 ; term of office of, 31 ;
    certain powers and duties of may be assigned, 31 ;
    effect of death of, 32 ; how assent of declared on
    reserved Bill, 33 ; legislative power of, 34 ; may
    remove certain judges, 34 ; power of as to Separate
    and dissentient schools, 34 ; Acts relating to powers
    of, 36, 39 ; when independent judgment of is
    called into requisition, 43, 80 ; instructions to, as
    to pardons, 204.
Governor, Lieutenant, by whom appointed and by whom
    removed, 34, 125 ; statutory powers of, 37, 39, 126 ;
    a corporation sole, 39 ; power of to assent to an Act
    of the Legislature, 121 ; Chalmers' opinion on power
    of to assent to such Act, 122, 130 ; position and
    authority of, 124 ; term of office of, 124 ; proceedings
    before removal of, 125 ; to whom answerable, 125 ;
    prerogative rights of, 126 ; Sir John A. Macdonald's
    opinion on appointment of, 127 ; Hon. Mr. Four-
    nier's opinion on powers of, 127 ; Justice Gwynne's
    opinion on position of, 128.
16

www.ingramcontent.com/pod-product-compliance
Lightning Source LLC
Chambersburg PA
CBHW020845270326
41928CB00006B/561